AF435868

SOUND HEALING

STEP-BY-STEP

How to use crystal and Tibetan bowls, tuning forks, voice, and shamanic drums to balance energy for physical, mental, emotional, and spiritual harmony.

MERCEDES CADARSO SÁNCHEZ

MARÍA SOCASTRO GONZÁLEZ

The Wing Book

1st edition: March 2026

Title: Sound Healing Step by Step

INDEX

I am thrilled to dedicate this book to my biggest fans, my dear sister Victoria Cadarso and my soulmate Luis Javier Ruiz. Thank you for always being there for me.

Mercedes

I especially dedicate this book to my parents and my husband for their unconditional support and constant words of encouragement. And to all those who accompany me, have accompanied me, or will accompany me in my life.

María

And we thank Pedro Espadas, who was our first editor and who encouraged us to share our experiences as sound therapists.

"The importance of sound is key because of its healing properties. I believe that sound can play a significant role, as it repairs imbalances in any physiological disorder. In my experience, sound is such a powerful instrument for relaxation and mind-body healing, as it touches and profoundly transforms the emotional and spiritual planes."

DR. MITCHELL GAYNOR, Director of the Department of Oncology Medicine at the Strang-Cornell Center in New York

PROLOGUE

When we began studying and practicing sound healing it was very difficult to find training courses and literature on the subject. The little information available was in English, and we slowly translated what we considered relevant. With our experience in consultations, we developed the manuals we used in our training courses.

It was our friend and then-editor, Pedro Espadas, who encouraged us to write a useful and practical book so that newcomers to this field could have an easy guide to begin working with sound safely and effectively. This would allow them to find well-being and harmony by learning, in a simple and effective way, the different applications of these sound vibrations through the various sound instruments currently available.

There are many instruments that can be used in sound therapy, but we have chosen those that we find most practical, easy to use, and effective. These are: the voice, Tibetan singing bowls, quartz crystal bowls, drums, and tuning forks. We understand that it's not common to have access to all the instruments discussed in this book, but once you've integrated the knowledge about how sound works in healing, you'll find that you can achieve similar results using any of these instruments. Therefore, we encourage you to start with the instrument that's most accessible to you and gradually add others to your sound therapy sessions.

With practice, we realize that each of us is more drawn to certain instruments than others, and those are the ones we feel most comfortable with, which is perfectly fine. Above all, it's important that we feel comfortable using each instrument, as this will facilitate the proper flow of energy throughout our bodies and lead to better results for ourselves and those who come to our sessions.

With experience, you'll discover that sound is a magnificent tool for finding your balance and will help you maintain the state of health we so desperately need right now. We believe that the sound vibrations we experience with these instruments can change our lives and, consequently, the lives of those around us, producing a chain reaction that helps improve and harmonize the world.

As quantum physics states, everything is in constant motion; each particle emits a vibration that affects others, and these in turn affect those adjacent to it. And if this is true, we have in our hands the necessary sound instruments to help us change our vibration and thus change the world around us.

We have written this book with great enthusiasm and with the hope that it will provide the appropriate techniques and knowledge so that those interested in helping others can use sound in their sessions to improve the various physical and emotional ailments that people bring to their practice.

This book can be used both for personal balance and for therapeutic work with others. Caring for our own center is fundamental to being able to support others, and sound is a simple, quick, and effective tool to promote this balance, whether for oneself or in a therapeutic setting. We firmly believe that health, harmony, and balance can be achieved simply, just as our ancestors did. They used the sounds of instruments and their voices to connect with their inner selves, while also protecting their bodies from illness.

We hope you'll be as excited by the sound as we are!

CHAPTER 1

THE BASICS OF SOUND PHYSICS

Since ancient times, in every corner of the planet we turn our attention to, sound has been present—both as a cultural expression and as a tool for healing. All traditions and philosophies, especially shamanic ones, have relied on the healing qualities of sound and music.

These traditions held that sound could influence the state of all our systems. It could affect us in many different ways: giving the body the strength it needs to heal, helping us find the emotional well-being that is sometimes so necessary, or even making us ill if we were exposed to sounds that were not harmonious.

In China, India, and in the Greece of Pythagoras, many texts explored the power of sound to heal and energize the body. In fact, these writings often expressed the idea that sound has the capacity both to destroy and to heal. One example is the Chinese *Hua!*—translated as "the roar of the tiger"—a shout taught in martial arts that, when combined with the force of a strike, can cause death by acting directly on the opponent's nervous centers.

For ancient Chinese culture, the voice was considered an expression of one's deepest being. Through the student's tone of voice, a master could discern whether the student was worthy of the teachings to come.

Based on the vocal quality of a newborn, it was believed possible to foresee whether the child's future would be marked by good or bad fortune. Likewise, the timbre of a person's voice was thought to reflect their state of health. For example, a nasal voice was associated with lung disorders, while a shouting or overly forceful voice was believed to indicate liver imbalance.

In later periods, the use of sound and traditional music evolved into more structured musical works, giving rise to what we now know as music healing. During the 1980s, sound experienced a renewed resurgence as a therapeutic tool, and today it is gaining increasing recognition—either as a healing in its own right or as a complement to other approaches.

From a scientific perspective, we can say that when we receive a sound stimulus, it affects the entire body. Skin, bones, and the auditory system all receive the vibration, which then travels throughout the organism, producing specific effects such as biochemical changes, balancing of neuronal activity, relaxation of the muscular system, among many others. These changes influence the whole body through both the nervous and circulatory systems.

According to psychiatrist and musician R. Benenzon (2000), "The vast majority of sound stimuli that impact the nervous system are processed at subcortical levels. This is why the use of sound is especially relevant in conditions that involve the nervous system, whether the origin is organic or psychological."

When we attend a concert, the sound vibrations produced by the voice and musical instruments interact directly with our bodies. These sounds can evoke images and memories, while rhythm naturally invites movement. All of this generates sensations—more or less pleasant—that trigger biochemical changes affecting the entire body.

But there is more. When we are exposed to the vibration of an instrument that is very close to us, or even in direct contact with the body, such as a crystal singing bowl or a tuning fork, the physical effects of that vibration have an even stronger impact on the organism.

Fabien Maman, a researcher into the effects of sound, observed that blood cells changed both color and shape when exposed to certain sound frequencies. In one particular case involving cancerous cells affecting the matrix, he found that specific sounds caused these cells to begin to break down. According to his own reports, these experiments suggest that sound vibration plays a decisive role in the transformation of cellular structure.

1.1 What Is Sound?

From a scientific point of view, sound is the result of the vibratory movement of a body. These vibrations cause molecules to move, and each molecule passes that vibration along, creating a chain reaction that our brain ultimately interprets as sound.

For a sound phenomenon to occur, three elements are required:

1. A flexible object capable of vibrating, such as a musical instrument or the human throat.

2. An elastic medium that can carry those vibrations, such as air.

3. A receiver that can interpret vibrations, such as the human ear.

From an energetic perspective, sound is a vibration that helps bring the body into harmony, influencing emotional, mental, and even spiritual states. Sound can help us move from sadness to joy, access altered states of consciousness or stabilize the heart rate.

It's important to distinguish sound from another element that, while not essentially musical, also affects the body: noise. Noise is a form of sound transmission without clear definition, made up of irregular vibrations that disturb and overstimulate the auditory nerve and, as a result, the body's systems as a whole.

Noise usually creates an unpleasant sensation and can even contribute to illness. For example, urban noise pollution often leads to anxiety and stress and can eventually result in sleep problems. Sound, on the other hand, tends to generate a sense of harmony, which is why we work with it—to harmonize the body's systems and support the restoration of health.

1.2 Transmission and Reception of Sound

One of the most effective ways sound is transmitted through the body is via the skeletal system, particularly the spine. Research has shown that the parts of the body that "listen" best and transmit vibration to the rest of the organism are the bones of the skull together with those of the spinal column.

As Ibarrola explains in *Music Before Birth*, (Música para antes de nacer) the fetus hears the mother's voice through the coccyx. For this reason, in an instinctive attempt to connect more deeply with her, the fetus positions its skull beneath the iliac crest, which acts as an extremely powerful resonance chamber, allowing the fetus to enter vibrational connection with the mother.

Sound is perceived simultaneously by the auditory system, the skin, the joints, the muscles, and the bones. Through the skin, it is possible to recognize certain vibrations even when the ear does not consciously register them. Not hearing a vibration does not mean it doesn't exist. This is why people with hearing difficulties are still able to "feel music" and receive the healing vibrations of sound.

Scientific studies have shown that in individuals with hearing impairments, tactile vibration activates brain responses in the auditory areas in the same way it does in people with normal hearing.

"A person does not perceive sound only through the ear; they listen through every pore of the skin. Sound penetrates the whole being and, according to its particular influence, it raises or lowers the rhythm of blood circulation, sharpens or calms the nervous system, and either awakens passions or brings about peace."
— Inayat, The Music of Life

Sound travels through solids and liquids more quickly than through gases. In sound HEALING, we work with all three forms of propagation, adapting them to the needs of each client.

When addressing physical issues, it's important to keep in mind that different parts of the body transmit vibration at different speeds.

STRUCTURE	M/S
Bone	4,080
Muscle	1,570
Blood	1,500
Fat	1,500

Because of this, we can say that when the issue is physical, the work should be applied directly through the bones and muscles. When the issue is emotional, however, we can work through the energetic and auditory systems.

1.3 Understanding the Qualities of Sound

Sound has certain qualities that define it, and it's useful to understand the terms used in both physics and music to describe the same concepts. As therapists, we will use both sets of terminology interchangeably.

MUSICAL QUALITIES	PHYSICAL QUALITIES
Tone	Frequency (pitch)
Volume	Intensity (wave amplitude)
Rhythm	Duration
Timbre	Timbre (waveform)

Tone or frequency

This quality allows us to classify sounds as high, low, or mid-range.

The more oscillations there are in one second, the higher the sound (higher frequency). Conversely, the fewer oscillations per second, the lower the sound (lower frequency).

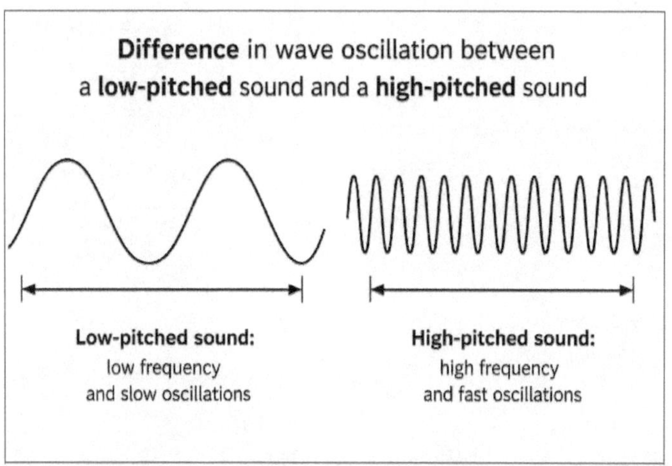

Volume or intensity

This refers to the strength with which a sound is produced and allows us to classify sounds as loud or soft, depending on the amplitude of the waves.

In the case of a Tibetan singing bowl, the harder it is struck, the greater its volume or intensity.

Rhythm or duration

This refers to the length of time a sound is heard, which can be long or short.

When we play a bowl continuously, we create a fast rhythm. To produce a slower rhythm, we leave more space between each strike.

Timbre or waveform

Timbre allows us to distinguish between two sounds that have the same intensity and the same frequency but are produced by different instruments.

For example, a "G" note played on a singing bowl and sung by the voice has the same frequency, but a different waveform, which allows us to distinguish between the two emitters.

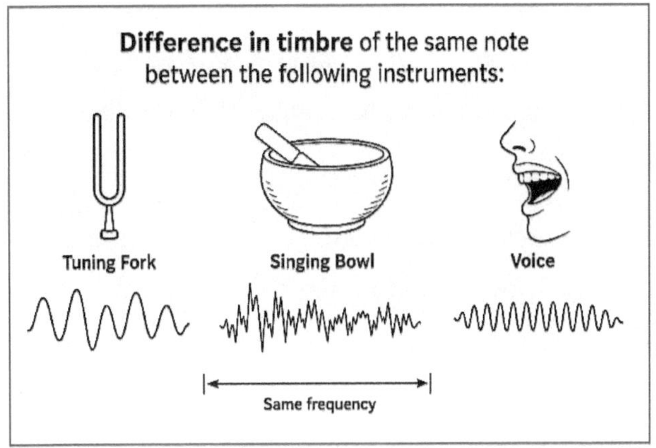

1.4 Resonance

Resonance is the natural vibration of an object. It is the specific frequency at which something vibrates. There are two main types of resonance:

Free resonance: This occurs when an object begins to vibrate after meeting a frequency that exactly matches its own. A simple example is using two tuning forks tuned to the same frequency. If one of them is struck and the other is placed close enough, the second tuning fork will begin to vibrate as well.

Forced resonance: This happens when a vibrating source causes another object to vibrate, even if they do not share the same frequency.

For example, the vibrations of a Tibetan singing bowl can cause the skin of a drum to vibrate, even though the two instruments are not the same.

From a therapeutic point of view, forced resonance gives rise to a phenomenon known as entrainment. This occurs when an object emitting strong vibrations alters the vibrations of another object, causing the second one to synchronize with the first so that both end up vibrating at the same frequency.

If an organ or a subtle field, such as a chakra, is not vibrating at its optimal frequency, a tuning fork corresponding to its healthy frequency can be applied and through entrainment—or what could also be called "vibrational memory"—the organ or chakra begins to vibrate again at its harmonious frequency, supporting the restoration of balance and health.

Sound healing is based on helping the body or an altered emotional state return to balance through the resonance produced by coherent or healing frequencies applied to the person. However, it is not only the frequency of sound that produces healing. The intention of the therapist also plays a key role.

Intention is the energy that underlies the sound. It is the state of awareness we hold when producing a sound. This awareness becomes encoded into the sound, travels with it, and is ultimately received by the person who hears and perceives it. From this we can conclude that healing occurs when all three phenomena take place, as shown in the following image:

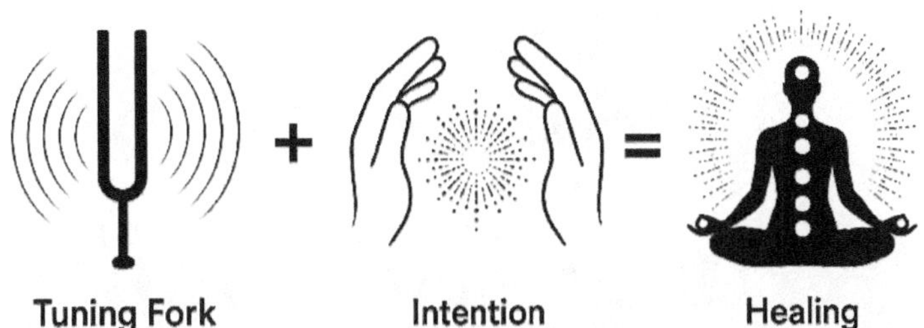

Frequency + Intention = Healing
Tuning Fork
Intention
Healing

CHAPTER 2

THE ENERGY BODY

Sound is energy, and as such, it can be used as a healing tool within what is known as Energy Medicine or Energy Therapies.

Energy Medicine is a systems-based approach to addressing illness. It draws on ancient medical traditions such as Chinese Medicine and Ayurvedic Medicine, which view human beings as energetic systems: we absorb energy, we emit it, we acquire it, and we transform it. This energy can be understood from two main perspectives:

- **A biological perspective**, where the focus is on the physical body.

- **An energetic perspective**, where attention is placed on how energy flows correctly through the body.

Traditional healing has historically focused on the physical system. In sound healing, however, the energetic system is essential, as it forms the foundation of this practice.

Each tradition or philosophy has explored the human energetic system from its own point of view and has developed techniques to help keep it in balance.

In the following sections, we will briefly review the three fundamental energetic systems—chakras, meridians, and the aura. However, to make learning and practical application easier within sound healing, we will focus primarily on one of these systems.

Everything is made of energy: cells, viruses, bacteria, medications, and even our thoughts and emotions. The human body is a complex energetic system, and illness is the result of energetic imbalances. From this perspective, health can be restored by bringing that energy back into balance.

Negative emotions created by traumatic experiences or limiting beliefs acquired during childhood—when they are not properly resolved—can create energetic blockages in the chakras. If these blockages are left unaddressed, they may eventually lead to significant illness, both psychological and physical.

For this reason, sound therapy works on multiple levels: physical, emotional, mental, and spiritual. By doing so, it allows energy to flow correctly again and helps restore harmony within the system. In sound healing, we use the principle of forced resonance to re-establish vibrational frequencies in each organ, emotion, and thought pattern.

For example, if we needed to work with fear related to exams, we would use healing frequencies that stimulate the third chakra to strengthen personal power, the seventh chakra to support memory, and at the same time work with the first chakra to help dissolve fear.

Healing intentions, together with the client's belief in the effectiveness of healing frequencies, supports the healing process. Intention and belief are therefore fundamental aspects of healing.

There are different energy systems within the human body, developed across various cultures. However, the most well-known and widely used in therapeutic practices are the chakras, meridians, and the aura.

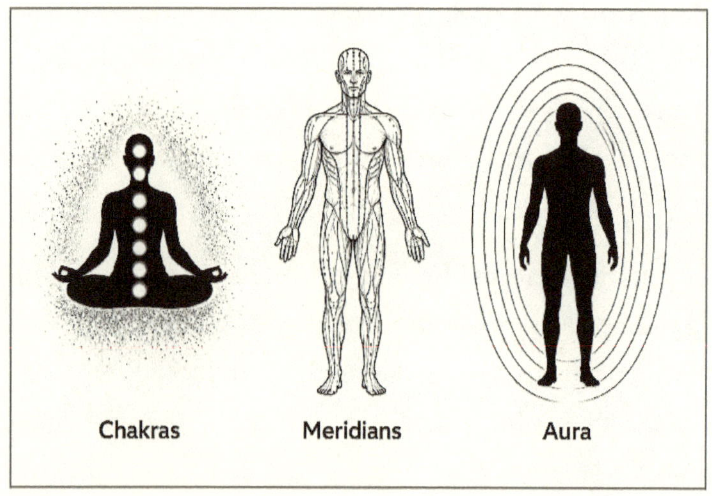

The Chakra System

Chakras are small energy vortices located along the spinal column. They are nourished by different vibrational frequencies.

According to the Hindu tradition, which dates back more than five thousand years, there are seven main chakras, traditionally represented as lotus flowers, each associated with the color of the frequency at which it vibrates.

Chakras distribute energy to the vital organs and to the rest of the body through energetic channels known as *nadis*, ensuring the proper functioning of the entire system.

The Meridian System

Traditional Chinese Medicine, which also dates back more than five thousand years, studied the system of energetic channels and named them meridians.

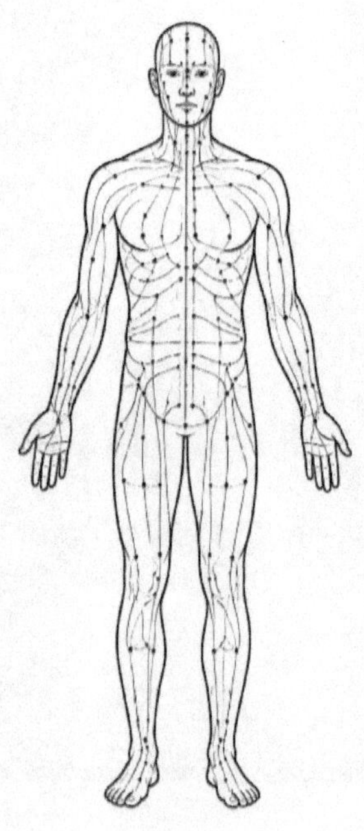

Along these pathways are energetic points that some traditions consider to be "mini chakras." These points act as regulators of energy for all the organs and systems of the body.

The Aura System

Those who study the aura describe it as an electromagnetic field that surrounds the body. Depending on the person's state of health, this field may extend only about fifty centimeters in times of illness, or several meters when the person is in a healthy state.

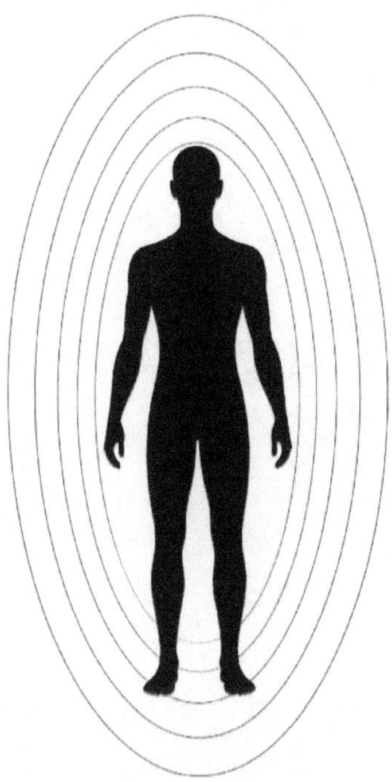

This energetic layer is created by the energetic emissions of the chakras and meridians. These three systems nourish each other and continuously influence one another. For the practical application of sound therapy, the system we will focus on is the chakra system.

CHAPTER 3

THE CHAKRA SYSTEM

Chakras are energy centers that are constantly in motion. The word *chakra* means "wheel" in Sanskrit. As each chakra spins, it pulses throughout the energetic field and provides vital energy for the functioning of the physical, emotional, mental, and spiritual bodies.

Each chakra vibrates at its own frequency and has a specific harmonic pattern that defines its unique function. It also resonates with other frequencies, such as a particular color, sound, essential oil, and so on.

Each chakra generates exactly the amount of energetic frequency it needs to perform its function, much like a light bulb requires a specific voltage to work properly. Chakras also act like parabolic antennas, receiving and transmitting frequencies as they are provided by the universe.

When pain or difficulties appear on a physical, emotional, mental, or spiritual level, the flow of energy in one or more chakras becomes altered, affecting different parts of the body.

As long as we are alive, the chakras remain active or open. However, when illness or energetic imbalance appears, they may function or emit energy either below or above their optimal level. In other words, chakras can be described according to how they are functioning:

Blocked / closed / low / slow / hypoactive

Open / balanced / normal / optimal

Overloaded / overactive / hyperactive

Keeping the chakras balanced is essential for increasing our energetic flow. The more freely energy circulates, the greater our sense of well-being—and as a result, the healthier and happier we feel.

Hindu tradition has passed down, for more than five thousand five hundred years, the knowledge of seven main chakras which, when properly developed, can help overcome illness and energetic disharmony.

Each chakra has its own characteristics and qualities, which complement the others. Together, they energize and help harmonize the different areas that make up our lives.

When energy flow is unbalanced, the chakras can be in two main states: overloaded or blocked.

An overloaded chakra is one that is overactive. Energy flows too quickly or in an unbalanced way, which can lead to hyperactivity in the physical, emotional, or mental areas associated with that chakra.

This often manifests as overwhelming emotions, extreme behaviors, excessive control, or energetic overstimulation. In this case, energy is circulating, but it does so without harmony or balance.

On the other hand, a blocked chakra is one in which energy does not flow or does so in a very limited way.

This generates energy deficiency that can be manifested as apathy, emotional disconnection, difficulty expressing needs, a feeling of stagnation, or even persistent physical symptoms. In this state, energy is retained or stagnated.

The goal of energy work with the chakras is not to indiscriminately activate energy, but to restore a balanced and coherent flow, allowing each energy center to fulfill its function within the overall system.

For this reason, we will now take a closer look at the characteristics of each chakra.

3.1 First Chakra: Root (Muladhara)

The root chakra marks the beginning of our story as human beings. This is where our sense of safety, belonging, well-being, health, and prosperity reside.

It is where we ground ourselves, and everything that unfolds in the body, mind, and spirit has its foundation here.

CATEGORY	DESCRIPTION
Location	Perineum in men, base of the uterus in women.
Glands	Gonads (testes and ovaries).
Associated psychological themes	Security, survival, procreation, financial matters, health, body image, and weight.

Associated anatomy	Legs, feet, hips, bones, large intestine, anus, skin, blood, excretory and urinary organs, skeletal system.
Physical issues associated with a blocked chakra	Eating disorders. Intestinal problems: constipation, cramps. Issues related to the bones. Skin disorders. Sciatica. Hemorrhoids. Degenerative arthritis. Insomnia. Blood or circulatory system disorders.
Psychological issues associated with a blocked chakra	Fear, insecurity, instability, anxiety, disorganization, undisciplined behavior, poor sense of self, dissociation from the body.
Physical issues associated with an overactive chakra	Obesity, overeating, sleeping too much, fatigue, low energy, clumsiness, slow and sluggish movements.
Psychological issues associated with an overactive chakra	Greed, materialism, addictions, overworking. Obsession with routines and security. Fear of change, strict limits.

3.2 Second Chakra: Sacral (Svadhisthana)

Everything we create, from a drawing or a poem to a powerful emotion, is generated by the energy that begins to flow from the second chakra.

This chakra governs creativity, sexuality, fertility, and our most intimate relationships. This is also where feelings happen.

CATEGORY	DESCRIPTION
Location	Lower abdomen, uterus.
Glands	Adrenal glands.

Associated psychological themes	Passion, emotions, desire, creativity, pleasure, sexuality, gestation, intimate relationships, enjoyment of life, joy.
Associated anatomy	Abdomen, uterus, ovaries, genitals, kidneys, bladder, lower third of the back, hip area, pregnancies.
Physical effects of a blocked chakra	Fertility problems, rigidity, impotence, bladder and kidney infections and stones, intermittent menstruation, pain in the lower back, miscarriages.
Psychological effects of a blocked chakra	Creative block, fear of commitment/relationships, emotional coldness, inability to have fun.
Physical effects of an overactive chakra	Sex addiction, premature ejaculation, urinary incontinence, heavy menstruation, excessive thirst.
Psychological effects of an overactive chakra	Bipolar personality disorder, excessive emotionality, sudden mood swings, hypersensitivity, addiction to pleasure and substances, emotional dependency.

3.3 Third Chakra: Solar Plexus (Manipura)

The solar plexus chakra is the center of our individuality, personal power, and self-worth.

When it is strong and balanced, we naturally radiate confidence, warmth, and reliability, attracting others through a healthy sense of humor and personal charisma.

CATEGORY	DESCRIPTION
Location	In the area located below the sternum.
Glands	Pancreas.
Associated psychological themes	Abundance, prosperity, laughter, self-esteem, our abilities, autonomy, envy, egocentrism, shame about oneself, desire to live.
Associated anatomy	Stomach, digestive organs, large and small intestines, back, pancreas, muscles, liver.
Physical effects of a blocked chakra	Low energy, chronic fatigue, poor digestion, diabetes, gallstones, impaired liver function, weak middle back.
Psychological effects of a blocked chakra	Low self-esteem, lack of willpower, victim mentality: blaming others for one's problems, inability to set boundaries, feeling of having no personality.
Physical effects of an overactive chakra	Hypertension, stress, ulcers, insomnia due to excess energy, addiction to physical exercise, strong appetite, physical symptoms related to stress.
Psychological effects of an overactive chakra	Anger, irritability, lack of self-control, obsession with power, materialism, excessive competitiveness, arrogance, insensitivity, oversensitivity, lack of sensitivity, narcissism.

3.4 Fourth Chakra: Heart (Anahata)

The heart chakra is the center of love, compassion, and meaningful connection, guiding our relationships with others and with ourselves.

As the bridge between the physical and spiritual chakras, it brings balance and harmony, allowing healing energy to flow naturally through the hands in a subtle yet powerful way.

CATEGORY	DESCRIPTION
Location	Heart area.
Glands	Thymus.
Associated psychological themes	Giving and receiving love, harmony, healing, compassion, self-love.
Associated anatomy	Heart, lungs, shoulders, arms, hands, chest, breasts, thymus gland, cardiovascular system.
Physical effects of a blocked chakra	Heart problems, respiratory issues, pain in the chest and arms, immune system problems, depression.
Psychological effects of a blocked chakra	Emotional coldness, intolerance, irritability and impatience, being overly critical of others, lack of compassion for others, dependence on others.
Physical effects of an overactive chakra	Depression, exhaustion, breast cancer, mastitis, benign breast lumps, low blood pressure.
Psychological effects of an overactive chakra	Putting others' needs before your own, victim mentality, dependency in relationships, emotional attachment, neglecting oneself, jealousy.

3.5 Fifth Chakra: Throat (Vishuddha)

The throat chakra is the first of the spiritual chakras, and together with the two above, belongs to the mental realm of vibration, visualization, intuition, and thought.

What you say, see, imagine, and what you think are all reflected in the upper chakras. And it all begins here, in the throat chakra, where your inner vibration is expressed through words, symbols, gestures, and expressions.

All the ways you communicate with your inner world, the outer world, and with the Divine.

CATEGORY	DESCRIPTION
Location	Throat.
Glands	Thyroid and parathyroid glands.
Associated psychological themes	Communication with oneself, others, and God; ability to express feelings; knowing how to listen; speaking and listening to the truth.
Associated anatomy	Throat, trachea, esophagus, neck, thyroid, cervical vertebrae, mouth, jaw, teeth, ears.
Physical effects of a blocked chakra	Lumps in the throat, laryngitis, pharyngitis, neck pain, hypothyroidism, hearing loss, tinnitus.
Psychological effects of a blocked chakra	Problems with self-expression, weak voice, fear of speaking, inability to say what you want, taking things too literally.
Physical effects of an overactive chakra	Hyperthyroidism, nodules on the vocal cords from speaking or shouting, pyorrhea, cavities, mouth ulcers.

<table>
<tr><td>Psychological effects of an overactive chakra</td><td>Talking too much and too loudly, interrupting, speaking without thinking, inability to listen to others, stating "your truth" without considering the other person's feelings (lack of assertiveness).</td></tr>
</table>

3.6 Sixth Chakra: Third Eye (Ajna)

The third eye chakra is the center of intuition, inner vision, and deep understanding beyond physical senses. It governs imagination, dreams, and the inner voice that guides what feels right or wrong.

When balanced, it allows wisdom and awareness to flow clearly, helping you perceive not just events, but their meaning.

CATEGORY	DESCRIPTION
Location	Between the eyebrows – center of the forehead.
Glands	Pituitary (hypophysis – master gland).
Associated psychological themes	Intuition, perception, wisdom, imagination, dreams.
Associated anatomy	Brain, nerves, forehead, eyes, nose, pituitary and pineal glands, carotid nerve plexus.
Physical effects of a blocked chakra	All related to the head: pain, migraines, nasal congestion, sinusitis, visual dysfunctions (blindness, astigmatism, farsightedness, cataracts…).
Psychological effects of a blocked chakra	Lack of imagination, weak intuition, poor decision-making, denial of reality, psychopathic behavior.
Physical effects of an overactive chakra	Headaches due to vein dilation, hallucinations, hyperventilation, cerebral hemorrhage, brain tumor, blows to the head.
Psychological effects of an overactive chakra	Inability to distinguish dreams from reality, disconnected from reality, being overly in the mind.

3.7 Seventh Chakra: Crown (Sahasrara)

The crown chakra connects us to universal energy and to something greater than ourselves.

It governs higher awareness, inspiration, and moments of deep insight that expand consciousness. Through it, we explore life's big questions about identity, origin, and purpose.

CATEGORY	DESCRIPTION
Location	Fontanelle.
Glands	Pineal gland.
Associated psychological themes	Knowledge and understanding, spirituality, connection with a higher power or universal energy, the soul.
Associated anatomy	Brain (especially the cortex), gray matter, central nervous system.
Physical effects of a blocked chakra	Learning difficulties, nervous system failure, migraines, autism, brain tumor, coma, amnesia, senility, Alzheimer's disease.
Psychological effects of a blocked chakra	Feelings of loneliness, depression, lack of inspiration, spiritual crisis.
Physical effects of an overactive chakra	Headaches, brain tumors, fainting.
Psychological effects of an overactive chakra	Obsession or addiction to spiritual or intellectual topics, hallucinations, nervous breakdowns, feeling "up in the clouds": over-intellectualization.

With this basic understanding of the chakra system, we can now begin to use sound as a powerful tool for healing and balance. Sound allows us to gently influence energy, restore harmony, and awaken the body's natural ability to realign itself.

At the same time, this is an invitation to explore more deeply one of the most profound energetic systems within natural medicine—one that has guided healing traditions for centuries and continues to offer clarity, well-being, and inner transformation today.

CHAPTER 4

THE THERAPEUTIC EFFECTS OF SOUND

4.1 The Energy of Sound

Sound accompanies us throughout our lives. It provides information about the environment we are in and, as a result, helps us understand it while influencing us in many different ways.

When it comes to the relationship between sound and healing, it's important to remember that although all sounds are made of vibrations, not all vibrations are healing.

As mentioned earlier, for a sound to be healing it must have a coherent frequency and be accompanied by intention—the conscious will of the person producing it—while the person receiving it must also be receptive to its effects. Since sound is used here as a healing tool, it's essential to understand it deeply in order to apply it correctly. For this reason, we will look at its therapeutic dimensions and characteristics.

Intensity

From a therapeutic perspective, the intensity of sound produces different responses. Low-intensity sounds tend to create feelings of calm, trust, and closeness, and are often deeply relaxing. In contrast, loud sounds stimulate and energize, generating sensations of vitality and strength—sometimes to the point of startling or even physically shaking us.

Duration

Long, sustained sounds tend to produce sensations of peace and calm. On the other hand, short sounds that follow one another without interruption create a sense of speed, which has an activating effect and can increase energy levels.

Timbre

We could say that, depending on each person's preferences, the different timbres of singing bowls or tuning forks can generate different states of mind. The cells of our body and our energy system recognize these timbres and respond accordingly.

In therapy, each client responds better to a particular timbre. Therefore, a person may react better to a frequency of 136.10 Hz emitted by the voice than to a tuning fork with the same frequency.

For this reason, we advise that before a session we show the client the different instrumental options so that they can intuitively choose the one that best enhances their healing, since, at an unconscious level, they already know the response.

Part of the secret power of sound lies in learning to control timbre; for example, the voice can create harmony or disharmony depending on how it is produced.

For instance, when we decide to be calm, we adopt a soft and relaxed timbre. When we want to be friendly, we adopt a light and kind tone, and when we are angry, our tone becomes dark and rigid.

With practice, we can learn to create physiological and energetic changes in ourselves and others by altering the timbre of various instruments to achieve the desired effects.

Rhythm

Continuing with the elements that make up sound, we find rhythm, its most primary and ancestral element. It is formed by the combination of sounds of different durations, silences, and accents.

Rhythm has the quality of connecting us with our own bodily cycles, such as breathing, pulse, wakefulness, and sleep… and with those of nature: days, tides, lunar phases, seasons…

Rhythm can stimulate us and incite us to move when it is fast, but it can also have a hypnotic and relaxing effect when it is slow and monotonous. Rhythm is applied therapeutically to everything related to physiological and organic aspects, helping to activate vital rhythms and promoting movement and motor stimulation.

It also helps us release energy when working with marked, fast-pulsing rhythms. And it acts in the opposite way when using soft, slow-pulsing rhythms.

Frequency

Regarding frequency, low sounds are considered to have a great relaxing power, since they resonate sympathetically with the first chakras (first, second, and third).

In contrast, high sounds activate the resonance of the upper chakras. As the sounds become increasingly higher pitched, they stimulate mental activity, aiding in learning. We can also say that high sounds can break down energetic-emotional blockages, which are the cause of illness.

The different frequencies are traditionally known as notes.

4.2 Musical notes and their properties

According to Pythagorean tradition, each sound possesses a specific vibration that corresponds to a number. From this idea, Pythagoras was able to assert that the cosmos is sound, because everything in our universe is in constant vibration.

Therefore, he stated that the vibratory motion of the planets produced a sound he called the "Music of the Spheres."

Researchers Favre D'Olivet and Schneider have established a series of correlations between musical notes and their healing properties. According to their research, we can draw several conclusions regarding the therapeutic properties of musical notes.

Fundamental musical notes act as stable and archetypal frequencies that generate direct resonance with specific structures of the physical, energetic, and emotional body.

Each note possesses a specific vibration that can influence specific organs, glands, chakras, and emotional states, promoting processes of balance, regulation, and harmonization.

When a fundamental note is emitted in a sustained and conscious manner, its vibration helps the organism remember its natural pattern of coherence, facilitating processes such as homeostasis, purification, emotional integration, and energetic stabilization.

For this reason, in sound healing, notes are used as tools to accompany physical, emotional, and energetic processes.

Why don't sharp notes have the same correspondence?

Sharp or flat notes (like C#/Db) don't represent a stable archetype in themselves but rather function as transitional frequencies between two fundamental notes.

Being situated at an intermediate point, their vibration doesn't consolidate a complete harmonic pattern, but instead acts on states of tension, imbalance, or disharmony.

For this reason, sharp notes don't work so much on structural harmonization, but rather focus especially on internal conflicts, unbalanced behaviors, or altered emotional states.

We could summarize by saying that:

- Fundamental notes tend to order, integrate, and harmonize.

- Sustained notes tend to mobilize, confront, and reveal imbalances.

Both are valuable in sound healing, but they serve different functions: fundamental notes maintain balance, while sustained notes help identify and unlock areas of conflict that need to be examined and transformed.

Next, we will delve deeper into the healing qualities of each note and its frequency

C (261HZ)

CATEGORY	DESCRIPTION
Basic survival energy	Courage, bravery, action and movement, energy recharge.
Chakra	Root.
Glands	Gonads.
Numerical correspondence	Number 1.
Organic correspondence	Bladder, reproductive organs, especially the male ones.
Color	Red.
Emotional states it works with	Paralysis, fear, terror, apathy, exhaustion, indifference, lack of trust in life, lack of initiative, sadness, feeling of not being grounded in life, lack of attention and concentration.
On a physical level, it harmonizes	Anemia, hypothyroidism, hypothermia, hypotension and anorexia, chronic fatigue syndrome, fibromyalgia, depression, states of shock and concussion. Works on the muscles of the feet and legs, strengthens bones and supports calcium metabolism. Enhances iron absorption.

C # OR Db

CATEGORY	DESCRIPTION
Organic correspondence	Kidneys
Energetic area	Between the first and second chakra
Color	Red-orange
Emotional states it works with	Works on impulsivity and difficulty reflecting or thinking. People who struggle to understand their own limits, behaviors, and actions.
On a physical level, it harmonizes	Supports regulation of the renal and adrenal systems. Favors detoxification and elimination processes, especially in cases of retention or overload. Supports recovery of physical balance after prolonged states of energetic depletion.

D (293HZ)

CATEGORY	DESCRIPTION
Basic survival energy	Flow and continuity. Supports homeostasis. Stabilizes energy. Aids nutritional assimilation. Balances emotional processes related to anxiety. Develops creativity. Supports the body's detoxification processes.
Chakra	Second
Glands	Adrenal glands
Numerical correspondence	Number 2
Organic correspondence	Reproductive organs, especially the female ones, and kidneys
Color	Orange

Emotional states it works with	Indecision, uncertainty, doubt, emotional withdrawal, shyness, jealousy, rigidity
On a physical level, it harmonizes	Sexual dysfunctions, male sexual impotence, frigidity, vaginismus, disorders of the reproductive organs. Supports recovery from depression, especially postpartum depression

D# OR Eb

CATEGORY	DESCRIPTION
Organic correspondence	Gallbladder
Energetic area	Between the second and third chakra
Color	Orange-yellow
Emotional states it works with	Difficulties accepting one's body design. People with a tendency to expect others to always solve their problems. Helps generate the inner strength needed to overcome difficult situations.
On a physical level, it harmonizes	Supports the functional balance of the gallbladder and adrenal glands, promoting a better response of the body to stress. It is an excellent tone that helps improve skin health.

E (328,8HZ)

CATEGORY	DESCRIPTION
Basic survival energy	Personal power. Helps develop self-awareness. Builds self-esteem. Unites body and mind. Balances excessive desires.
Chakra	Third

Glands	Pancreas
Numerical correspondence	Number 3
Organic correspondence	Stomach – Spleen
Color	Yellow
Emotional states it works with	Lack of interest in life, apathy, indifference. Difficulty finding direction. Greed and excessive ambition. Works with processes of resentment, bitterness, and guilt.
On a physical level, it harmonizes	Balances metabolism. Helps prevent infectious diseases. Supports digestive difficulties. Diabetes. Pancreatitis. Stimulates cellular regeneration in the treatment of degenerative diseases (osteoarthritis, arteriosclerosis, Alzheimer's). Helps in cases of constipation. Muscle contractures.

F (348,3HZ)

CATEGORY	DESCRIPTION
Basic survival energy	Connection with love. Levels and balances energy. Increases understanding. Develops integration between body and emotion. Expands awareness of others. Fosters autonomy.
Chakra	Fourth
Glands	Thymus
Numerical correspondence	Number 4
Organic correspondence	Heart

Color	Pink
Emotional states it works with	Restlessness. Distress. Feelings of victimhood. Works on abandonment trauma. People with self-destructive tendencies. Distrust. Oversensitivity. Suspicion. Impatience. Irritability.
On a physical level, it harmonizes	The heart, shoulders, arms, and lungs. Supports cases of allergies, colds, bronchitis, and asthma, especially in situations related to high blood pressure. Back pain and disturbances in respiratory and cardiac rhythm.

F# OR Gb

CATEGORY	DESCRIPTION
Organic correspondence	Hepatic system and gallbladder
Energetic area	Between the fourth and fifth chakra
Color	Pink–Blue
Emotional states it works with	Stimulates communication both inwardly and outwardly. Helps dissolve excessive ambition and greed. Works on hypocrisy. Balances feelings of inferiority. Develops tolerance. Supports emotional isolation caused by lack of communication.
On a physical level, it harmonizes	Supports liver and gallbladder function, promoting detoxification processes. Contributes to balance within the autonomic nervous system. Encourages the secretion of digestive enzymes, aiding fat digestion.

G (391,1HZ)

CATEGORY	DESCRIPTION
Basic survival energy	Development of expressiveness. Communication. Encourages the energy of sharing.
Chakra	Fifth
Glands	Thyroid
Numerical correspondence	Number 5
Organic correspondence	Throat
Color	Blue
Emotional states it works with	Communication difficulties. Excessive talkativeness. Feeling misunderstood or unheard. Develops hearing and the capacity for listening.
On a physical level, it harmonizes	Supports food metabolism. Thyroid disorders and ear, nose, and throat conditions. Releases tension and unlocks cervical contractures. Stimulates regulation of body temperature. Helps tissue renewal.

G# OR Ab

CATEGORY	DESCRIPTION
Organic correspondence	Lungs, respiratory system, and skin
Energetic area	Between the fifth and sixth chakra
Color	Blue–Purple

Emotional states it works with	People with a tendency to idealize others. Helps self-expression in front of others. Releases fear of being observed and criticized. Develops personal opinions and supports finding one's own identity.
On a physical level, it harmonizes	Supports lung function and deep breathing. Contributes to strengthening the immune system. Helps improve oxygenation of the body. Regulates calcium and phosphorus metabolism.

A (438,9HZ)

CATEGORY	DESCRIPTION
Basic survival energy	Connection with wisdom. Supports synchronization between mind and body. Encourages cooperation with others. Helps cultivate presence in the "here and now."
Chakra	Sixth
Glands	Pineal gland
Numerical correspondence	Number 6
Organic correspondence	Brain
Color	Indigo
Emotional states it works with	Lack of connection with the body. Contradictory emotions. People without their own opinion who are easily influenced by others. Develops intuition, allowing connection with inner wisdom beyond intellectual reasoning.
On a physical level, it harmonizes	Acts directly on pain. Balances brainwaves. Encourages connection between the cerebral hemispheres. Helps

	reduce epileptic activity. Also supports improvement in migraines and headaches.

A# OR Bb

CATEGORY	DESCRIPTION
Organic correspondence	Central nervous system, brain, pineal gland, and higher neuroendocrine system
Energetic area	Between the sixth and seventh chakra
Color	Indigo–White
Emotional states it works with	Helps people who tend not to always tell the truth. Supports integration of spirituality into daily life. Works with tendencies toward self-deception, lack of clarity in decision-making, or energetic dispersion. Releases fixed or obsessive thoughts. Supports endogenous depression. Helps clarify sexual identity.
On a physical level, it harmonizes	Supports balance within the central nervous system. Contributes to regulating sleep–wake cycles. Helps relieve tension headaches associated with mental overload. Promotes a sense of clarity and mental rest.

B (492,7HZ)

CATEGORY	DESCRIPTION
Basic survival energy	Purpose and meaning in life. Develops objectivity and intellectual organization. Supports energetic connection with the universe. Connects with our spiritual dimension. Enhances effectiveness.
Chakra	Seventh

Glands	Pituitary gland
Numerical correspondence	Number 7
Organic correspondence	Neocortex
Color	White
Emotional states it supports	Lack of connection with others due to arrogance. Desire for power and control over everything and everyone. Selfishness. People who always try to impose their ideas on others. Develops the capacity for detachment and integrates the overall energetic system.
On a physical level, it harmonizes	Regulates the body's water–salt balance. Supports proper functioning of the pituitary gland.

4.3 Melody

Melody is another element of music. We can define it as a succession of notes at different pitches linked to a rhythm.

Melody has an immediate effect on the emotional aspect, as it has the capacity to provoke and evoke countless sensations, feelings, and memories. Listening to a melody connects a person with their entire emotional world.

Therefore, melody has a great therapeutic capacity, as it not only helps to understand and express the affective universe, but does so in an orderly way.

4.4 Harmony

Harmony is the most complex and refined element of music. It is formed by the combination of all the previous elements: sound, rhythm, and notes. Harmony can be defined as the simultaneous sounding of tones or notes.

Many instruments used in sound healing can produce simultaneous sounds, such as Tibetan and crystal bowls or tuning forks. The human voice is primarily a melodic instrument, but it can easily create harmony when several people sing together or when it is combined with other instruments.

Within harmony, we can distinguish the following:

Harmonic Intervals

Harmonic intervals occur when two sounds of different pitches are heard at the same time. These intervals can be created when playing several instruments together. For example, when a low note is played on a Tibetan singing bowl while a high note is played simultaneously on a crystal bowl.

Within harmonic intervals, we also find chords, which are groups of more than two sounds sounding at the same time. In this case, chords are heard when a crystal bowl, a Tibetan bowl, and the voice are all emitting different notes simultaneously.

Consonance and Dissonance

When frequencies sound simultaneously, they create sonic combinations that can feel more or less pleasant.

A harmonic interval is the simultaneous sounding of two notes. When the result is pleasant, it is called consonance; when it is unpleasant, it is called dissonance.

Consonance is considered a state of rest and balance, while dissonance creates a sensation of tension and conflict.

From a therapeutic perspective, both are useful and necessary, as they represent the two poles of an experience that needs to be felt.

Once the client has experienced release or unblocking through dissonant sounds, we then introduce consonant sounds to help restore balance.

4.5 Benefits of Sound Intervals

These are some of the basic properties traditionally attributed to sound intervals in sound therapy.

Fundamental Interval or Unison: C–C

- Helps connect with the energy of the Earth, a connection necessary for releasing both physical and emotional toxins and pain.
- Slows down internal rhythms, supporting deep rest.
- Often used for its strong grounding effect.
- Brings structure and a sense of safety into life.
- Supports circulation in the legs, helping prevent and reduce ankle edema.

Second Interval: C–D

- Helps initiate action.
- Connects us with our creative power.
- Used to generate movement and release stagnant energy.
- Supports constipation by helping mobilize and eliminate toxins from the body.
- Helps prevent and reduce stretch marks in the abdominal area.
- Relieves menstrual pain and helps release gas.
- Activates kidney energy, supporting proper drainage.
- Works simultaneously with the qualities associated with the first and second chakras.

Third Interval: C–E

- Balances anxiety and worry.
- Develops personal power grounded in the connection with the Earth, generating a stronger and brighter emotional response.
- Supports digestion and nutrient metabolism.
- Releases tension in the lower back and dorsal area.
- Helps with stomach conditions such as ulcers, gastritis, and gastroenteritis.
- Works with aspects associated with the first and third chakras.

Fourth Interval: C–F

- Develops connection with self-love.
- Encourages forgiveness.
- Releases tension in shoulders and arms.
- Cultivates compassion and understanding for oneself and others.

- Helps uncover one's personal truth, strengthened through the grounding energy of the first chakra.

Fifth Interval: C–G

- Helps improve communication.
- Supports the expression of needs and desires.
- Works effectively with colds, pharyngitis, laryngitis, and ear pain.
- Develops the voice and both inner and outer listening. Releases tension in the neck and helps relieve cervical contractures.
- Works with aspects associated with the first and fifth chakras.

Sixth Interval: C–A

- Supports connection with inner wisdom. Encourages the development of intuition
- Helps with migraines, temple pain, and pressure behind the eyes.
- Releases states of constant worry.
- Brings flexibility to ideas and thought patterns, offering a broader view of reality.
- Works with aspects associated with the first and sixth chakras.

Seventh Interval: C–B

- Enhances memory and intellectual development.
- Supports neuronal connection and communication between brain hemispheres.
- Helps find the "door" toward resolving a problem.
- Strengthens psychic qualities and spirituality.
- Supports proper energetic flow throughout the chakra system.

- Works with aspects associated with the first and seventh chakras.

Octave Interval: C–C

- Brings stability.

- Supports connection with the Higher Self.

- Encourages presence in the "here and now" and personal transformation.

- Supports resolution and personal and spiritual evolution.

Despite how complete this list may seem, sound therapy is an ever-expanding and constantly evolving art. For this reason, it is important to experiment with ourselves, to explore how each sound or interval affects us, what changes it brings about, and what emotions it evokes—without fear of making mistakes. When the intention is healing, that healing energy always prevails.

CHAPTER 5

THE VOICE

Through our voice, we interact with the world. We express our emotions and desires, and we can sense when someone is angry, happy, unwell, or content. Spoken voice, singing, and the sounds we make—laughter, crying, sighs—all convey our personality and how we are feeling in each moment.

For example, when we are happy, our voice tends to sound higher and brighter. When we are sad, the voice becomes lower, duller, almost abandoned and lacking strength.

The effects of the voice are wide-ranging, influencing us on physical, emotional, mental, and spiritual levels. The voice can modify brain waves, balance communication between the hemispheres, reduce stress levels, regulate blood pressure, relax muscles, and, above all, stimulate our innate capacity for self-healing.

In modern society, the habit of singing and verbal expression has largely been lost. In the past, there were songs for every moment of life. Daily activities were accompanied by music: lullabies, harvesting songs, planting songs, spring songs. Through these, our ancestors maintained a greater sense of physical and emotional balance.

Our body knows how to distinguish between beneficial and harmful sounds produced by the voice and responds accordingly, even if we are not always consciously aware of these effects until a physical or psychological response appears.

There is no voice without air, and the voice is the first instrument we possess—and the most natural one. Several parts of the body are involved in vocal production, especially the respiratory system, the vocal apparatus, and part of the digestive system.

When we speak of vocal emission, or phonation, we are referring to both spoken and sung voice. Both use the same mechanisms for production, although singing, due to its specific characteristics, engages the respiratory and vocal systems in a more precise and focused way.

It is important to understand that we all have the ability to sing within us. We simply need to reconnect with our creativity and move beyond the shame that limits us in order to find our vocal expression.

Whispering, humming, chanting, sobbing, shouting, or whistling are all expressions that can support self-healing and the healing of others. If we pause to listen to ourselves, we will notice that each of us naturally sings and produces sounds spontaneously as a way of balancing our own energy.

When we are tired, we naturally rebalance ourselves by yawning. When we feel angry, we release and harmonize through shouting. When we are in pain, we soothe ourselves with a moan. Sadness is expressed through crying, and joy through laughter.

Any instrument capable of producing sound can be used as a healing tool. However, it is most common to work with the instruments that have traditionally been used for healing—those we want to share with you in this book.

Beyond learning how to use these instruments, it is essential to have a basic understanding of hearing and breathing. To carry out an effective sound healing session, whether using the voice, tuning forks, or crystal bowls, both hearing and breathing are fundamental. They are essential tools for healing others and ourselves.

5.1 The Ear

Let us begin by understanding the basic functioning of the auditory system, since the ear—along with sight—is one of the primary organs through which we relate to our environment.

Even in the womb, hearing is the first sense to develop and the one that allows us to establish our earliest contact with the outside world. The fetus needs only a few weeks to begin perceiving the first acoustic signals, such as the mother's voice or the sound of her heartbeat.

The essential role of the auditory system is to capture and process sound stimuli generated both in our environment and within our own body.

5.2 Noise and Illness

The range of hearing varies from person to person. One of the factors that influences it is the aging process. Under ideal health conditions, a human being should be able to perceive frequencies ranging from 16 to 20,000 hertz.

Due to the sensitivity of the human ear, it requires constant care. While hearing allows us to connect with the environment, excessive acoustic stimulation can have harmful effects—not only on hearing itself, but also on the mind and overall health.

In many cases, constant acoustic stimulation is used to avoid feelings of loneliness or to compensate for a lack of communication between people. Unfortunately, this continuous exposure to sound is harmful to the ears, which gradually become damaged over time.

In the long run, excessive sound or noise is not comforting at all—quite the opposite. When noise levels exceed 90 decibels, the cells of the inner ear begin to suffer damage, which sooner or later leads to a reduction in hearing ability. Below is a list of common sound intensity levels found in our environment:

- **20 dB:** the ticking of a clock

- **25 dB:** whispering

- **50 dB:** a quiet conversation

- **60 dB:** a hotel room with the television on

- **70 dB:** a loud conversation

- **80 dB:** a busy street

- **90 dB:** the sound of a moving truck

- **100 dB:** a crowded restaurant

- **120 dB:** nightclubs, rock concerts

Noise has been shown to cause the following problems:

- Nervousness

- Stress

- Anxiety

- Sleep disturbances and insomnia

- Fatigue

- Sudden emotional changes and depressive states

- Immune system disorders

- Circulatory system disorders

- High blood pressure

5.3 Hearing protection and auditory hygiene

There are many ways to protect our ears and prevent damage to our hearing ability. It's important to remember that many forms of ear damage are irreversible.

Below are some protective measures to help keep your ears healthy:

1. The louder the music, the less time we should listen to it. After one hour of listening at a high volume, we should rest our ears for at least forty-five minutes.

2. Avoid listening to music through headphones at excessive volume. Headphones deliver sound directly into the auditory system, which can be very harmful to hearing and may also affect overall health balance.

3. If we want to listen to music, it's best to use a good-quality sound system. The clearer and more precise the sound, the less auditory stress it creates.

4. If we frequently visit places with loud music, we should protect our ears. Cotton earplugs can be useful, as they reduce the frequency range without significantly compromising sound quality—unlike silicone earplugs.

5. When turning on the radio or television, try lowering the volume until you notice the point at which sounds become difficult to understand. Practicing this regularly can help improve auditory sensitivity.

6. If you live in a large city or on a busy street, installing double-pane windows is advisable. Prolonged exposure to noise pollution interferes with proper rest and can eventually contribute to illness.

7. When showering or swimming, make sure excessive water does not enter the ears. Using earplugs is recommended, as water exposure can increase the risk of eardrum perforation.

8. Noise and stress are not the only factors that harm hearing. Stimulant substances are also a risk factor. Various studies indicate that excessive alcohol, coffee, or nicotine consumption can damage the sensory cells of the inner ear.

5.4 Exercise to Train Your Hearing

Below are several exercises and guidelines designed to help you develop your listening ability. These exercises can also be practiced by—or recommended to—clients who come to your practice with mild hearing difficulties.

Hearing Loss Self-Assessment

Take a moment to answer the following questions:

- Do you have difficulty following and understanding conversations when several people are speaking?

- When you go to the theater, can you only understand the dialogue when you are seated in the front rows?

- Do you find it difficult to hear the ticking of a clock?

- Does sound feel weaker in your left ear compared to your right ear?

- When talking on the phone, do you often ask the other person to speak louder so you can follow the conversation?

- Do you frequently ask people to repeat words or phrases you didn't clearly understand?

- When you are walking and a car approaches, do you hear it only at the last moment?

- Have you stopped hearing high-pitched sounds such as crickets or birds singing?

If you (or your client) answered "yes" to several of these questions, there may be some degree of hearing loss. To determine the extent of the loss, it is advisable to consult an ear, nose, and throat specialist (ENT), who can carry out specific tests to assess the level of impairment.

Close Your Eyes and Open Your Ears

Sit comfortably in a chair and close your eyes. Bring your attention to all the acoustic signals you are able to perceive and try to remember them. After a few minutes, notice whether the sounds become clearer or whether you begin to hear sounds you did not perceive at the beginning.

It can be helpful to write down the sounds you notice during the exercise. When you repeat it later, compare your notes and observe whether there has been any change in the number or intensity of the sounds you perceived.

Variation

To further develop auditory perception, wear cotton earplugs while doing household tasks, reading a book, or working on the computer.

Keep the earplugs in for about three hours. When you remove them, notice how your hearing sensitivity has increased.

Note: Do not perform this exercise while driving, walking in the street, or at work where safety is a concern, as it could lead to accidents.

5.5 Breathing

The primary function of the respiratory system is to bring oxygen into the lungs, transfer it to the bloodstream, expel waste substances, and regulate body temperature. At the same time, it is the main foundation that supports the voice.

During the breathing process, the body absorbs oxygen through the respiratory organs—the nose, mouth, pharynx, larynx, trachea, bronchi, and lungs—and then distributes it through the blood to the body's cells. For this reason, we can say that cellular energy depends on breathing.

The billions of cells in our body can only be properly energized when we breathe freely and deeply, which also allows for the effective elimination of toxins and waste products.

Breathing movements also express and reveal emotions. Some experts have found that deception can be detected through variations in breathing patterns.

Breathing gives us valuable information about our physical and emotional state, as bodily reactions and emotional responses are closely linked and influence one another.

Breathing changes depending on the emotion we are experiencing; each emotion is accompanied by a specific breathing pattern.

Thanks to this connection, we can help balance our emotions by practicing certain breathing dynamics. To do this effectively, it is essential to develop and maintain a posture that allows breathing to occur correctly.

5.6 Postural hygiene for proper breathing

The essential foundation for healthy vocal emission and fluid breathing is good body posture—one in which joints and muscles are relaxed and free from tension.

Let's first look at the most common postural mistakes that can limit breathing:

- Forward projection of the cervical vertebrae; chin lifted.

- Jaw positioned too far forward or too far back.

- Shoulders rounded forward or lifted upwards, excessive curvature of the upper back.

- Collapsed sternum or an excessively lifted chest.

- Lateral shift of the hips consistently to the same side; locking the knees backward.

- Uneven distribution of body weight on the feet.

You may recognize several of these patterns in yourself or in a client. There's no need to worry or feel overwhelmed. What matters most is understanding that for change to occur, we first need to acknowledge that there is something worth changing.

Once we become aware of the bodily habits we want to change, we can reconnect with our sense of vertical alignment. This allows us to introduce new adjustments that support healthy breathing and a correct, fluid vocal emission.

Our body is naturally drawn downward by the Earth's gravity, which calls for an alignment that distributes body weight evenly. To sense this, imagine an axis running straight through the center of your body, dividing it evenly from right to left and from front to back.

The body's weight flows equally down both legs and rests firmly on the feet, which are grounded on the floor.

When both feet receive the same load, muscles maintain the right level of tension and no muscle group becomes overloaded.

Proper posture does not imply rigidity—quite the opposite. It allows for energetic flow, relaxation, flexibility, and balance.

Through the below QR you will have direct access to a video demonstrating the correct posture for singing and a series of body relaxation exercises that are very helpful for releasing muscular tension and, at the same time, developing body awareness.

It also includes additional content designed to support your path in sound healing and to offer tools that can make a real difference in your early practice.

You can also access it from this link:

https://thewingbook.com/bonus/sound_therapy/

Practicing it also gives us valuable information about our energetic and physical blockages, helping us better understand ourselves and strengthen our sense of presence in the "here and now."

Once correct posture has been established and integrated into the body, and before exploring the different types of breathing, we would like to address a question that always arises in our classes:

5.7 Breathe through your nose or your mouth?

There are many techniques and schools that offer different guidelines on this topic. Some claim that breathing through the mouth is not advisable, while others promote techniques that combine both nasal and oral breathing.

In reality, both pathways are possible, and each has its advantages and disadvantages, which we will outline below.

Breathing through the nose

- The air is warmed and humidified by the nasal mucosa.

- Dust and harmful environmental substances are filtered out.

- Bacteria are neutralized by enzymes present in the nasal passages.

- The endings of the olfactory nerve are stimulated.

- It takes longer to fully fill the lungs with oxygen.

Breathing through the mouth

- Air enters with less resistance and reaches the lungs more quickly, allowing large volumes of air to move rapidly.

- Deep breaths are easier to achieve, which is helpful during intense physical activity or for singers and wind instrument players.

- Airflow is easier to control than with nasal breathing.

- The air enters cold and unfiltered.

As we can see, both types of breathing have their benefits and limitations. From a natural standpoint, we should generally aim to breathe through the nose, especially for those living in highly polluted cities. However, in many situations, particularly when singing or working with specific therapeutic goals, mouth breathing may be used intentionally to access certain physical, energetic, and healing advantages.

5.8 Chanting and intoning

Chanting and intoning use sounds that help balance our energy. In fact, they can even release deeply held traumas that lie at the root of many illnesses and discomforts.

To practice intoning, you don't need to know how to sing, have studied music theory, or even have a "beautiful" voice. Anyone who can speak can intone and use their voice as a powerful tool for health and well-being.

When we finally decide to use our voice as a healing instrument, certain vocal challenges may arise and create insecurity.

Below are some of the most common difficulties:

Running out of air

This can be caused by several factors:

- Injury to the respiratory system due to illness or long-term smoking.

- Blockage or tension in the chest muscles.

- Using an excessive amount of air while singing.

- Tension or blockage in the muscles that control exhalation.

Difficulty producing sound

This usually happens when we are nervous. In these cases, inhalation becomes blocked in the chest. Air builds up under pressure, which closes the larynx and makes sound production impossible.

Air loss during intoning

This occurs when air escapes while we are speaking or intoning, and it can have several causes:

- Collapse of the chest during exhalation.

- Long-term misuse of the vocal cords.

- Presence of nodules or polyps on the vocal cords.

Shallow inhalation

This creates the sensation of running out of air and occurs when the upper chest is excessively expanded, blocking the lower abdomen.

Hoarseness

Hoarseness is caused by a narrowing of the vocal cords, which vibrate as air passes through them. This usually happens when the muscles of the larynx are tense instead of relaxed, preventing air from flowing freely.

In the QR code below, you'll find five carefully designed breathing exercises to help you develop conscious, deep, and functional breathing. These exercises will allow you to expand your lung capacity, refine your body awareness, and prepare your energy system, creating a solid foundation for later using your voice as a therapeutic tool in healing processes.

Breathing is the bridge between the body, emotions, and sound. By training your breath, you not only breathe better, but you also open the way for your voice to become a conscious channel for healing.

You can also access it from this link:

https://thewingbook.com/bonus/sound_therapy/

5.9 Vocal cord health and hygiene

Repeated patterns of poor vocal use can lead to irreversible damage. Below are some guidelines to help care for your voice:

Avoid harmful substances

Remember the damage caused by smoking, such as bronchitis, chronic pharyngitis, and shortness of breath, especially over the long term.

Frequent alcohol consumption also seriously harms the vocal cords.

The increase in blood pressure caused by certain foods—such as processed meats, coffee, sugar, chocolate, and alcohol—leads to increased blood flow to the vocal cords, which negatively affects intonation and can even result in voice loss.

Avoid overusing the voice

It is advisable to avoid frequent coughing or throat clearing. Instead, yawning is very beneficial, as it relaxes the throat, as is swallowing slowly.

Avoid shouting and speaking in noisy environments such as bars or nightclubs. Do not sing beyond the notes that feel comfortable for you.

Avoid holding your breath while thinking about what to say, as this creates unnecessary tension in the throat.

Do not speak in sentences longer than your natural breathing rhythm allows. Avoid clenching your teeth or jaw, and do not tense the tongue.

Maintain a healthy environment

Avoid using your voice when you are ill (colds, pharyngitis, laryngitis) or excessively tired.

Never ignore prolonged symptoms of vocal cord tension, such as hoarseness, voice loss, pain, or throat irritation. In these cases, consult a doctor, especially if symptoms last longer than fifteen days.

Avoid eating foods that are very salty, overly sweet, or excessively dry, as they cause dryness in the mouth and throat irritation.

Also avoid foods that increase mucus production, such as dairy products and their derivatives. Most importantly, drink adequate amounts of water to keep all vocal mucous membranes well hydrated.

5.10 Exercise to develop your voice

Find Your Inner Note

You can do this exercise sitting or standing, but always with your back straight.

- Cover your ears with the palms of your hands.
- Inhale and exhale deeply while trying to perceive the sounds produced within you.
- After a few minutes, you will perceive a repeating sound. That is the inner note at which you vibrate.
- Next, try to reproduce it with your voice and experience the sensations that come from connecting with your inner frequency.

Repeat this sequence five times.

Connecting with Your Voice

Find a quiet place and sit down.

- Close your eyes and don't cross your hands or feet.
- Take several deep breaths.
- Once relaxed, choose a note and sing it using the consonant "m".
- Try to perceive the energy it contains.

- When you have finished producing the sound, inhale slowly again and repeat.

- After a while, imagine you are sending sound energy to specific parts of your body.

Repeat this as many times as you like.

This exercise will activate your voice, allowing you to develop its healing potential.

5.11 Healing techniques through voice

Next, we will explore some voice healing techniques that you can use both on yourself and when supporting others.

These practices are designed to use the voice consciously as a vibrational tool, capable of influencing the physical body, the energy system, and the emotional state. Through sound, intention, and presence, you will learn to create spaces for listening, regulation, and harmonization.

The techniques presented below do not require advanced vocal skills, but rather attention, sensitivity, and inner coherence, allowing the voice to become a natural channel for support and healing.

Before carrying out any of the voice healing practices, it is essential to create an appropriate framework to support the therapeutic process. This involves, first and foremost, consciously preparing the space: a clean, tidy, calm, and energetically balanced environment fosters relaxation, openness, and a sense of security for the person receiving the session.

Similarly, it is essential to conduct a preliminary interview with the client, using clear and respectful questions to help you understand what they are going through, what aspects they wish to work on, and their current life stage.

This conversation will not only allow you to guide the session more precisely but will also help the client connect with their purpose, intention, and inner disposition before beginning the sound work.

The therapist's personal preparation is equally important: being centered, present, with conscious breathing and a clear intention, ensures that the voice and sound are used from a place of coherence and respect.

All these aspects, the preparation of the space, the preliminary interview, the guiding questions, and the essential recommendations before a session, are explained in detail in the QR code shared above, so you can integrate these practices in a solid, professional, and conscious way into your therapeutic work.

5.12 Vowels for balancing the chakras

Once the client interview has been completed and you have a clear understanding of the issues to work on, have the client lie down and invite them to take several deep breaths to relax both body and mind.

Next, place your hands over the area of the first chakra, about 15 centimeters (6 inches) above the client's body, and begin chanting the vowel "U," which corresponds to the first chakra. Maintain the intonation for at least three minutes.

Then move your hands to the second chakra and chant the vowels "UO." Continue this process with the remaining chakras, as explained below:

1. **First chakra:** Chant a low sound—the lowest tone you can comfortably produce—using the vowel **"U,"** for as long as needed.

2. **Second chakra:** Once you sense that the first chakra is balanced, move to the second and chant using the vowels **"UO."**

3. **Third chakra:** When the second chakra feels balanced, move to the third and chant the vowel **"O."**

4. **Fourth chakra:** Harmonize by chanting the vowel **"A."**

5. **Fifth chakra:** Harmonize by chanting the vowels **"AE."**

6. **Sixth chakra:** Harmonize by chanting the vowel **"E."**

7. **Seventh chakra:** Harmonize by chanting the vowel **"I."**

When chanting in an ascending direction, we are introducing the energy of the Earth. When we return in a descending direction, we bring the energy of the universe into the chakra system, preparing the pathway for Kundalini energy to flow.

In addition, all the systems and organs associated with each chakra benefit from receiving these two energies—feminine and masculine.

The process described above is intended for general balancing or harmonization. If there is a specific condition to address, for example, gastroenteritis, the vowel corresponding to the **third chakra** should be chanted for a longer period, **at least six minutes**, to support cellular restructuring.

5.13 Frequencies for balancing the chakras

Following the same procedure as in the previous exercise, we can use the different frequencies associated with the seven chakras to help bring the client into balance.

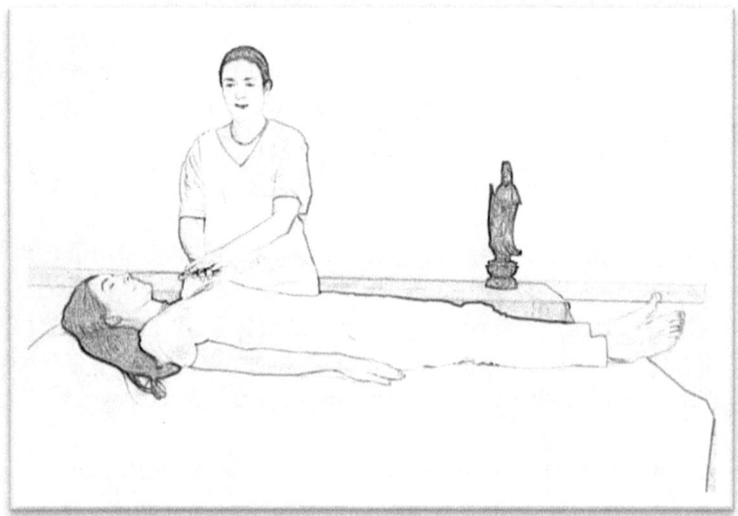

If we have a musical instrument available—such as tuning forks from the harmonic series—we can extract the different tones and intone them using our own voice.

To chant these frequencies, you can use the vowel **"A,"** as it acts as a bridge between body and mind energy:

1. **First chakra:** chant the frequency corresponding to the note **C (Do)**.

2. **Second chakra:** chant the frequency **D (Re)**.

3. **Third chakra:** chant the frequency **E (Mi)**.

4. **Fourth chakra:** chant the frequency **F (Fa)**.

5. **Fifth chakra:** chant the frequency **G (Sol)**.

6. **Sixth chakra:** chant the frequency **A (La)**.

7. **Seventh chakra:** chant the frequency **B (Si)**.

- This frequency-based approach is recommended for general energetic balancing.

When working with a specific issue, such as askin condition, it is important to first balance the energy by starting at the first chakra and moving up to the seventh, chanting the sequence from C to B.

Next, we apply the specific tones—in this case, D♯ (Re♯)—and finish by chanting from B to C, allowing the energy to descend from the seventh chakra to the first. By following this sequence, the mobilized energy is integrated and grounded in the root chakra, ensuring that the client leaves the session fully grounded.

In summary, to treat a skin condition, we could chant the D♯ frequency for six to ten minutes and then intone the sounds corresponding to each of the seven chakras, moving through both an ascending and descending sequence.

Once the entire process has been completed, we end the session by chanting the mantra "Om" for about three minutes to seal the energy of the work.

5.14 Mantras for Balancing the Chakras

The word "mantra" comes from Sanskrit, the ancient language of India, and is composed of "man," meaning "to think," and "tra," meaning "instrument." Mantras are used in various philosophies, cultures, and religions, with Hindu mantras perhaps being the most widely used in healing.

They involve the repetition of syllables or words that possess a specific vibrational power and aim to balance and heal the human being.

In this technique, we use mantras associated with each chakra. The therapeutic application follows the same process as in the previous techniques:

1. **First chakra:** Chant a low sound using the mantra **LAM** for as long as needed.

2. **Second chakra:** Once the first chakra feels balanced, move to the second and chant the mantra **VAM.**

3. **Third chakra:** When balance is sensed in the previous chakra, move upward and chant the mantra **RAM.**

4. **Fourth chakra:** Chant the mantra **YAM.**

5. **Fifth chakra:** Chant the mantra **HAM**

6. **Sixth chakra:** Chant the mantra **SHAM**

7. **Seventh chakra:** Chant the mantra **OM**

The session is completed by chanting the mantra **"Om"** for about three minutes to seal the energy of the process.

Remember that if there is a specific issue affecting one chakra, the corresponding mantra can be applied for a longer period to address the condition before continuing with the overall healing process.

5.15 Case Example

Abraham, a thirty-five-year-old high school history teacher, came to therapy to address the anxiety he experienced due to losing his voice during classes. For this reason, he decided that the most appropriate therapeutic approach for him would be voice-based healing.

A coworker had told him about the positive results they had achieved through voice therapy.

During the first session, Abraham described how he imagined himself standing in front of thirty teenagers who were "ignoring him," seemingly uninterested in anything he had to teach them. As the class progressed, he would gradually lose his voice until he was unable to speak at all.

We explained that the fear he was experiencing was primarily associated with the third chakra, linked to personal power. He commented that he had no physical symptoms that clearly pointed to this, but we clarified that the blockage in this chakra was critically affecting the fifth chakra, blocking it to such an extent that he would sometimes lose his voice for several days.

Because of this, he feared being fired for not being able to teach, which in turn created anxiety about not being able to support himself. This final concern gave us important information: the first chakra was also seriously affected.

After this conversation, we began the healing and decided to apply the chakra balancing technique using mantras, working especially with the mantras associated with the third, fifth, and first chakras.

The session lasted approximately one hour, during which childhood emotions surfaced. Feelings of having not been emotionally attended to by his parents. In that moment, Abraham discovered the root of his discomfort.

He left the session feeling relieved by this insight, and we agreed that he would return the following week.

When he came back, he told us that he was still experiencing voice loss, but the anxiety it caused had decreased, as he now understood the origin of the problem. However, a deep resentment toward his parents had surfaced.

We then applied the same protocol as the previous week, adding work with the specific mantra for the heart chakra in order to address the resentment.

During this session, Abraham cried uncontrollably. In fact, we had to pause and give him space to release all the pain he had been holding inside. Once he had calmed down, we continued with the session and agreed to meet again the following week.

When he returned, he shared that his fear of losing his voice had significantly diminished. We conducted one final session to help fully integrate the change. We also encouraged him to continue practicing the mantras he had learned during the sessions, especially whenever he felt even slightly insecure.

A few months later, one of Abraham's coworkers came to our practice with a similar issue and told us that Abraham was now feeling happy. His students' performance had improved as well, thanks to the fact that he had begun teaching them to chant mantras before class.

This practice helped structure the group's energy in a more harmonious way, allowing learning to be more easily integrated.

CHAPTER 6

TIBETAN SINGING BOWLS

It is said that along the caravan routes of Asia, goods were not the only things being transported for trade. Knowledge and religious traditions also traveled these paths. Shamans journeyed south through Mongolia, while Buddhists crossed the Himalayas northward from India. In Tibet, shamanism and Buddhism met.

Both traditions make extensive use of sound in their rituals and meditative practices. Their most common instruments include gongs, bells, dungchen horns, and bowls.

It is believed that the origin of Tibetan singing bowls lies in their use as offering vessels, making them very common in monasteries. There are also written accounts describing bowls being used as eating vessels. It is possible that the metal alloys of the bowls helped compensate for deficiencies in essential minerals in the diet. For example, a woman who had just given birth might eat from these bowls to absorb their healing properties.

Today, Tibetan singing bowls are increasingly well known in the West. Curiously, however, if one travels to Tibet, very little information about them is found there. Their origin is lost in time.

Eva Rudy Jansen, in her book *Singing Bowls*, recounts the experience of the Hungarian shaman Joska Soos in a lama monastery in England:

"They took me into a small room, and there were the bowls. I listened to them. Among the lamas themselves, these bowls were only used in secret rituals by those recognized as true masters of sound. They have learned to chant the ritual songs and to play the ritual instruments perfectly. They use the singing bowls in secrecy and only for themselves—never in public, not even for other monks.

It is strictly forbidden to speak about the rituals or about the singing bowls themselves. This is because knowledge of sound carries great power. If you were to ask a lama holding a singing bowl whether it is true that they are used for psychic, psychological, and physical purposes, he would smile and reply: Perhaps."

There are bowls originating from Mongolia, Siberia, Japan, Nepal, Vietnam, India, and China. Although their roots lie in the Himalayan region, they began to reach the West after the Chinese invasion of Tibet in 1951.

As explained by Enrique Carriedo in his book *The Bells of Shambhala*, one of the Dalai Lama's advisors researched the origins of Tibetan singing bowls and concluded that many of them were kept in monasteries without knowing exactly what they were used for. Their most common uses were meditation, astral travel, and interdimensional communication.

Stories tell that some bowls were forged through rituals performed during solar and lunar eclipses. Others say that the monks themselves created the bowls while chanting mantras with very specific intentions, which became imprinted in the metal and were activated each time the bowl was played.

6.1 Types of Tibetan Singing Bowls

Stellar–Manipuri

These bowls are said to be made from materials originating from stars (meteorites). They are recognizable by the dots along the rim and a star engraved on the bottom.

The star indicates the moment of completion of the bowl, and it is at that time that its energy is believed to manifest at its fullest—although, of course, they can be used at any time.

These bowls allow for deep soul journeys. They are used to reach states of illumination, to discover who we truly are, and to break energetic and emotional blockages.

Himalayan bowls

These bowls are made from melted stellar bowls. They are distinguished by their slightly outward-flaring rim and are mainly used to harmonize and ground the soul, as well as to clear blockages in the chakras.

When a Himalayan bowl is played, the frequency we hear causes energy to begin rising through the central energetic channel that runs along the spine, where the seven main chakras are located. As the energy ascends, it balances all the chakras, allowing the vibration to integrate into the body and transform into healing energy.

Mortuary bowls

These bowls are composed of iron, nickel, and bronze. They were traditionally used to hold the ashes of a cremated lama. During funeral rituals, the bowl was struck and the ashes were released, facilitating the energetic departure of the lama's soul.

The darker spots on the bowl indicate how many lamas it has held, the darker markings, the more lamas. These bowls are also used in healing practices to help release dense energies that have remained stagnant and blocked in the body.

Shambhala and Tibetan bowls

Their purpose is to heal the physical, emotional, energetic, and spiritual aspects of the human being. They also help us connect with our inner self, supporting personal evolution and the recognition of our inner divinity and wisdom.

Traditionally, Tibetan bowls were made with seven metals, although today—due to cost—they are often made with three or five. Within this group, we find the Shambhala Tiger bowl, which was heated to shape it and then cooled in snow. This process creates dark markings resembling tiger skin.

Chalice or grail bowls

The sounds of these bowls recharge the listener with energy. The external lines, besides being decorative, indicate that they work on bodily fluids. If they have internal circles, this means they help cleanse all the nadis.

Thado bowls

These are joyful-sounding bowls made from stellar material. They are used for healing, calming and relaxing the mind, and clearing stagnant energy.

Water or master bowls

Their sounds stimulate the body's healing potential and support the connection between the two cerebral hemispheres.

There are two types:

- Sun bowls, which correspond to low, positive sounds

- Moon bowls, which correspond to high, negative sounds

Ladakh bowls

These bowls are made in Nepal and have no interior or exterior markings. They are lightweight and can float on water due to air bubbles incorporated into the alloy during casting.

Their sounds attract luminous angelic energy and soothe the soul. They work on the physical body at a molecular and cellular level. Their deep vibration relaxes muscles and heals the heart.

Dolphin bowls

So named because, when activated with water, they emit sounds similar to dolphin calls. They are made with gold inlays and are used to harmonize all bodily systems.

"Black" or carbon bowls

Finished in aluminum and bronze, these bowls do not produce a wide range of harmonic sounds. Their tones ground and stabilize energy, activating the healing response in the person.

6.2 Other Tibetan Healing Instruments

Bells and Dorjes

The Tibetan bell represents feminine energy. This sacred instrument is usually paired with its counterpart, the dorje, which represents the masculine principle.

Both tools have been used since ancient times in Tibet and, like the bowls, are made from a combination of the seven metals associated with the chakras.

By combining these two elements—feminine and masculine—states of illumination can be reached. The bell releases blocked energy, while the dorje transforms it. For this reason, they are often used together. Both balance yin and yang energies and can dissolve energetic blockages.

When working with both instruments at the same time, the dorje is held in the right hand and the bell in the left.

When used separately, the Tibetan bell can be played by gently striking it or by sliding a wooden mallet along its outer rim to produce a sustained vibration.

The bell can be activated over each chakra and kept vibrating to help release negative energies that may be blocking them, thus preventing the onset of illness.

The sound of bells can also harmonize the nervous system and heart rhythm. It strengthens the immune system, reduces stress, increases endorphin levels in the body, and supports cellular-level healing.

It is also widely used to balance and purify spaces, dissolving dense energies that tend to accumulate in the corners of rooms. For this reason, it can also be used to cleanse our workspace after a session.

Tingshas

Tingshas (or tingshags) are connected by a leather strap and are activated by gently striking their edges together. The sound they produce helps you connect with your inner awareness, supports recognition and remembrance of who you are, and enhances consciousness and attention.

They are paired according to their tone and are handcrafted using ancient molds that are thousands of years old. They are made with seven metal alloys, such as iron, copper, silver, lead, bronze, tin, and traces of gold. Their thickness and shape play an important role in the creation of harmonics, helping the mind clear negative thoughts.

Tingshas are traditionally used by Tibetan monks to signal the beginning and end of meditation.

They feature different designs and Tibetan symbols engraved in the metal, such as the mantra Om Mani Padme Hum, the Eight Auspicious Symbols, dragons, and other sacred motifs.

These instruments have been used throughout regions such as Nepal, Tibet, and India for healing, meditation, relaxation, purification, awakening inner wisdom, prayer, mantra chanting, ceremonies, space-clearing rituals, aura harmonization, purification of body and mind, and during the dying process to help ease the transition into the next state as peacefully and harmoniously as possible.

6.3 Therapeutic properties of Tibetan bowls

Among the therapeutic properties of singing bowls, we can highlight a wide range of benefits on the physical, emotional, mental, and spiritual levels.

Physical Benefits

- Regulate menstruation and relieve pain

- Help drain varicose veins

- Support the release of repressed emotions

- Effective for headaches, muscle pain, and back pain

- Help regulate blood pressure

- Relax the body in cases of lower back pain

- Relieve digestive issues

- Help combat fibromyalgia and chronic fatigue

- Useful for sleep disorders

Energetic Benefits

- Dissolve energetic blockages in the chakras

- Stimulate creativity

- Enhance mental clarity

- Support a healthy childbirth process

- Facilitate personal growth and evolution

- Promote proper energy flow and the connection between chakras and meridians

- Balance the electromagnetic field

- Restore the aura

- Recharge the energetic system

Emotional Benefits

- Reduce anxiety and distress

- Effective in managing stress

- Support emotional balance in cases of depression and sadness

- Helpful for sleep problems

- Assist in working with hyperactivity in both adults and children

- Improve concentration and creativity

- Calm and quiet the mind

Spiritual Benefits

- Clears dense areas within the aura

- Brings inner peace and connection with inner wisdom

- During the dying process, supports the soul in its transition

- In coma states, helps invite the being either to return or to pass on in a calm and peaceful way

- Increases the sense of well-being by harmonizing and balancing all body systems

- Helps access deeper levels of being

- Encourages altered states of consciousness

6.4 Material composition and its benefits

These instruments are made from alloys of the **seven sacred metals**, traditionally associated with the planets of our solar system:

Table of correspondence between metals, chakras, and planets:

METAL	CHAKRA	PLANET
Lead	Muladhara (First chakra)	Saturn
Tin	Svadhisthana (Second chakra)	Jupiter
Iron	Manipura (Third chakra)	Mars
Copper	Anahata (Fourth chakra)	Venus
Mercury	Vishuddha (Fifth chakra)	Mercury
Silver	Ajna (Sixth chakra)	Moon
Gold	Sahasrara (Seventh chakra)	Sun

The metals were collected, melted, purified, forged, and shaped by hammering. This composition of seven sacred metals allows for a wide range of harmonic sounds and vibrations that sustain over time, expanding into the surrounding space and altering the energetic vibration of everything that comes into contact with their sound.

Each of the metals used to make Tibetan singing bowls has its own specific healing properties. When the bowls are activated, these properties are transmitted into the environment and received by those who listen.

It is important to clarify that the properties described below are energetic. These metals should never be ingested physically, as they are highly toxic. However, the energetic potential generated when a bowl is activated produces deeply healing effects.

Below are some of the best-known energetic properties of each of the seven metals:

Lead

- Helps define the boundaries of the ego.
- Encourages self-control and inner calm.
- Structure and stability to the skeletal system
- Useful in cases of chronic constipation.
- Supports conditions such as progressive muscular dystrophy.
- Helpful with polio-related issues.
- Enhances motor coordination.
- Useful in cases of deep fear or terror.
- Releases muscle contractures.

Tin

- Effective for back pain.
- Supports bone fracture healing.
- Improves joint flexibility.
- Helpful in cases of arthritis.
- A powerful energetic balancer.
- Stimulates compassion and empathy.
- Encourages kindness and sound judgment
- Helps find coherence, and inner alignment.

Iron

- Provides the strength needed to carry out personal projects.
- Facilitates oxygen transport through the blood.
- Stimulates the desire to live and enjoy life.
- Helps regulate anemic states and chlorosis.

- Useful in degenerative processes affecting organs.

- Helpful in cases of hypersensitivity.

- Enhances blood circulation.

Copper

- Strengthens sexual energy

- Supports processes of self-acceptance

- Important for detoxification processes in the body

- Useful in cases of multiple sclerosis.

- Supports gestation processes.

- Helpful in the treatment of tuberculosis.

- Regulates hormonal systems, particularly in hyperthyroidism.

Mercury

- Governs the nervous system, thought processes, and language.

- Effective for throat conditions and ear infections

- Helps prevent allergic processes.

- Stimulates proper digestion

- Helps combat halitosis.

- Useful for vertigo.

- Supports dietary regulation processes.

Silver

- A conductor of heat.

- Symbolically reflects fertility.

- Useful in cases of epilepsy.

- Effective for gastritis.

- Helps regulate diabetes.

- Helps prevent migraines.

- Supports attention deficit disorders.

Gold

- Symbolizes solar energy.

- Acts as a powerful energy conductor.

- Transmits vitality, strength, and confidence.

- Enhances self-awareness.

- Stimulates the nervous system.

- Used in treatments to alleviate rheumatism.

- Supports depressive processes.

- Helpful for anemia and pneumonia.

- Useful in cases of cancer.

- Supports vascular health.

- Helps prevent degeneration of the nervous system.

Important to note: Some people drink water that has been placed inside Tibetan singing bowls, but this practice is not recommended.

Traditional bowls are made from alloys of various metals, including mercury and lead, which can be harmful to health when they come into contact with water.

For this reason, Tibetan singing bowls should be used exclusively as vibrational and sound instruments and should not be used as containers for drinking liquids.

6.5 How to Choose a Tibetan Singing Bowl

No two Tibetan singing bowls are the same. Each one differs in weight, diameter, wall thickness, height, rim shape, and metal composition. Each metal produces its own sound, and even bowls made with the same metals can sound different depending on their proportions.

Many bowls made today are mass-produced on a lathe, but for healing work it is best to choose **handcrafted bowls**, such as traditional Tibetan or Shambhala bowls. If you can have the opportunity to touch and play different bowls, you will notice that each one carries a distinct energy.

Choosing your bowl should never be rushed. Take the time to hold it in your hands, play it, feel its weight, sense its unique energy, observe its color and shape.

When you feel something special as you activate a bowl—when your heart tells you *this is the sound*—you have found your healing bowl.

Once you have chosen your bowl, run your finger around the outer rim several times to charge it with your energy. Then play it, listen carefully, and observe your sensations. Bring it close to your chakras and notice the effects it has on your body.

You can experiment by activating it with both hands, using different mallets or strikers, observing how the sound changes, how far the vibration travels, and whether you can extend that vibration throughout your body.

6.6 Bowl size and its effects

Another important factor to consider when choosing a bowl is its size:

Small Bowls (7, 9, 12, and 15 cm)

These produce high-pitched, intense sounds. They are highly energetic and primarily stimulate the **upper chakras** (fifth, sixth, and seventh).

Their sharp harmonics help quickly and easily dissolve energetic knots and blockages, especially on emotional and mental levels.

Medium Bowls (16 to 20 cm)

These are ideal for balancing and harmonizing the **third, fourth, and fifth chakras**. They also help dissolve energetic blockages and facilitate the integration of mental and physical energy, supporting balance between the brain hemispheres.

Large Bowls (21 cm and above)

The largest bowls have a dual capacity:

1. They work on grounding and connecting with the Earth, helping to drain any harmful energy from the body, such as stress and anxiety.

2. They keep us in the "here and now," allowing energy to flow freely through the chakras.

If we have a large bowl available, we can benefit from a wide range of harmonic sounds, as these bowls are capable of producing low, mid, and high harmonics, depending on the mallets or strikers used to activate them.

For example, to bring out the main low tone, we use a cotton-headed mallet. To work with mid-range harmonics, we strike the bowl using a wooden mallet covered with felt. To activate only high-pitched sounds, we use a plain wooden striker.

As you can see, with a single large bowl you can already begin sound healing work, since it contains the capacity for all three harmonic ranges (low, mid, and high). Over time, you can gradually add more bowls, enriching the soundscape and the healing vibrations.

6.7 How to activate a bowl

When we speak of activating a bowl, we are referring to the mechanical action of striking or rubbing it with the appropriate tool.

Below is an overview of the tools, such as mallets and strikers used to activate the bowl's sound.

Rubber-tipped mallet

Used exclusively for striking. It mainly activates mid-range sounds and produces more vibration than audible sound. Suitable for healing sessions

Wooden mallet

Used only for striking. It activates high-pitched sounds exclusively and produces very little vibration in the bowl.

Leather- or felt-covered mallets

Used for gentle striking or rubbing. They activate mid-range sounds while maintaining a soft, continuous vibration.

Cotton-headed mallets

Used exclusively for striking. Ideal for healing, as they activate the bowl's low tones and generate deep vibrations that easily penetrate the body.

6.8 Types of wood used for mallets

When working with Tibetan singing bowls, it's important to consider the quality and type of wood used to make the mallets. Not all woods transmit vibrations in the same way, nor do they all produce the same type of sound in the bowl.

The density, hardness, and finish of the wood directly influence the sound response, the duration of the sound, and the quality of the vibration, fundamental aspects when the bowl is used for therapeutic purposes.

Choosing the right mallet not only improves the sound but also fosters a more harmonious, precise, and respectful experience with both the instrument and the person receiving the session.

- **Hard woods** (beech, teak, walnut, holm oak, oak): activate metallic sounds.

- **Soft woods** (pine, poplar, boxwood): activate deep or softened metallic sounds.

- **High-quality woods** (juniper, sabina, mountain pine, century-old beech): produce rich, well-balanced harmonic sounds.

- **Poor-quality wood**: produces sounds with little or no healing potential.

6.9 Activating and holding the bowl

The bowl is associated with feminine energy, while the striker or mallet represents masculine energy. When masculine energy transmits the necessary impulse, the feminine energy is activated, creating the sound vibration that initiates the healing process.

The bowl is supported from below and played from the upper edge. To produce sound, it can be struck with a striker, a mallet, or even the hand. The choice of striker or mallet depends on the bowl and on the type of sound or vibration you wish to obtain.

The striker is held like a pencil, while the mallet is struck against the side of the bowl. Remember: the thicker the striker, the deeper the sound.

Let's review the different ways to activate a bowl:

Methods of activation

Striking: Performed using a mallet or striker. The closer to the rim the bowl is struck, the higher the sound produced. Conversely, striking closer to the base produces a deeper tone.

Rubbing or Circling: Performed with a wooden striker, with or without felt or leather covering. The bowl is activated by rubbing the upper rim with a slight tilt, using consistent pressure and speed.

If the bowl squeaks, increase the pressure and slow down the rotation. If the sound becomes too loud, gently touch the rim with a finger to slightly reduce the volume without stopping the vibration.

Ways to hold a singing bowl

There are several ways to hold a singing bowl.

You can choose the one that best suits the situation, the healing technique you are applying, or simply the one that feels most comfortable to you:

1. Resting it on the open palm of the hand, making sure your fingers do not touch the bowl so the vibration is not dampened.

2. Holding the bowl with your fingers.

3. Placing it on a support, such as a cushion or wool base.

4. Placing it directly on your body or on another person's body.

Finding a bowl tuned to an exact musical note is rare, as bowls are handmade. Each bowl has a unique sound that evolves over time and in relationship with you. The more you play it, the more harmonics are activated.

If you allow yourself to feel its sound with your eyes closed, you may notice how the sound energy takes the form of a rising spiral, influencing both the surrounding space and everything that comes into contact with its vibration.

6.10 Directions of rubbing and striking

Another fundamental aspect of working with Tibetan singing bowls is the direction in which they are activated.

The way the bowl is struck or rubbed, as well as the direction of the movement, directly influences the quality of the sound, the projection of the vibration, and the energetic experience generated.

Considering the direction of activation allows us to work more consciously, precisely, and coherently, respecting both the instrument and the therapeutic purpose of the session.

Clockwise Rubbing

When the bowl is rubbed clockwise (to the right), energy is activated and inner perception expands. From a healing perspective, this movement balances and strengthens the electromagnetic field, introducing restorative vibrational energy.

Counterclockwise Rubbing

When the bowl is rubbed counterclockwise (to the left), healing energy is drawn inward to cleanse and unblock. At a therapeutic level, this helps release dense or stagnant energies within the body.

Ascending Striking

When the bowl is struck in an ascending direction (from feet to head), stagnant and dense energy is released from the body. Combined with a fast rhythm, this helps break biological-level energy blockages.

With a slow rhythm, it works more deeply on emotional blockages that have become crystallized in specific organs or body areas.

Descending Striking

When the bowl is struck in a descending direction (from head to feet), healing energy is introduced into the body, helping to harmonize all systems.

With a slow rhythm, the energy penetrates at a cellular level. With a fast rhythm, it energizes the body's structures.

6.11 Cleaning Tibetan singing bowls

The first care to give your bowl after acquiring it is to rub it inside and out with a piece of lemon, then rinse it thoroughly with water. Dry it immediately with a cotton cloth.

You can also cleanse and recharge the bowl by leaving it overnight under the full moon, preferably placed on the earth. If you feel the bowl has accumulated negative energy, placing it on the ground will help discharge it.

If you practice or teach Reiki, you can also use this method to cleanse your singing bowl. After any of these cleansing methods, hold the bowl in your hands for several minutes so your energy can integrate with it. You may also perform this simple ritual:

1. Once the bowl is clean and dry, sit in a comfortable place, light a white candle and some incense.

2. Hold the bowl in your lap and mentally thank it for being part of your life.

3. Express your joy for having this sacred object as one of your healing tools.

4. For the next few days, place the bowl on your bedside table so it remains in contact with your electromagnetic field and absorbs your energy.

Another periodic care is to smudge the bowl with incense smoke, helping to remove any residual energy left after a healing session. For wooden strikers, apply a few drops of olive oil using circular motions on the part that comes into contact with the bowl, until the wood feels fully nourished and impregnated.

Next, rub the striker with a cotton cloth to remove any excess oil that may remain on its surface. This simple care will help prevent the strikers from cracking overtime.

6.12 Exercise with singing bowls

Before beginning to apply sound healing with Tibetan singing bowls to future clients, it is essential that we, as therapists, personally experience the healing qualities of these instruments.

For this reason, the following practices are designed to help you develop an energetic bond with your bowl and to become intimately familiar with its sound. This is essential, as it will allow you to recognize when a client's system is out of balance, since the sound of the bowl will change and provide valuable information about the treatment to apply.

Feeling the sound vibration

Find a place where you won't be disturbed and where there isn't much noise.

- Hold the bowl in your left hand and rest it on your palm, making sure your fingers don't touch the base. This allows the vibration to flow freely, with as few obstacles as possible.

- Begin by activating the bowl with the cotton-tipped mallet. Strike the bowl in different areas and with varying intensities to feel how the sound and vibration change.

- Once you are familiar with these sounds, close your eyes and perceive the vibrations and sounds again. Observe whether anything has changed.

- Open your eyes, hold the bowl only with your fingers, and repeat the previous steps.

- Close your eyes again and observe how your sensations differ.

- Repeat the process using a different striker, such as one covered with leather. Hold the bowl on the palm of your hand and activate it in different areas and with different intensities.

- Close your eyes and strike the bowl again with the leather-covered striker, allowing yourself to feel the sounds and vibrations.

- Hold the bowl with your fingers and experiment once more.

- Then observe how a wooden striker activates different harmonics and vibrations.

Note: Remember that you can change hands—hold the bowl with your right hand and activate it with your left. Observe how the sensations change.

6.13 Sound union and energy self-balance

Find a place where you won't be disturbed and where there isn't much noise.

- Sit comfortably with the soles of your feet together. Place the singing bowl on top of it and activate it by striking or rubbing it with different mallets or sticks, feeling the vibrations pass through your feet.

- Then lie down and place the bowl on your root chakra. Activate it and allow yourself to feel the different vibrations, listening attentively to the sounds your bowl emits.

- Now place the bowl over the second chakra, activate it, and feel.

- Then position it over the third and fourth chakras and experience the vibrational sensation.

- Sit comfortably again, hold the bowl with either hand, position it at the level of the fifth chakra, and activate it. Repeat the same process with the sixth chakra.

- Now place the bowl on top of your head, holding it with one hand to prevent it from falling, and gently activate it with the striker.

It is recommended not to activate the bowl for too long or too strongly on this chakra, as it may cause discomfort or dizziness.

Once finished, repeat the same process in a descending direction. As described earlier, ascending movements release and unblock energy, while descending movements introduce new and renewed vibrations.

After completing the process, take a few minutes of silence and relaxation to allow the vibrations and sounds to fully integrate into all your chakras. When you feel ready, slowly return to an upright position and drink a glass of water. If you wish, you may eat a small piece of dark chocolate, as this helps you ground yourself and return fully to your physical body, from which we often disconnect when working with sound.

6.14 Healing techniques with singing bowls

As we have seen throughout this manual, the sound of Tibetan singing bowls is considered a holistic healing tool within the field of energy therapies. It can be applied as a standalone session or as a complement to other therapies such as massage, aroma therapy, and others.

Using the sound of the bowls, we can perform a chakra test, since the sound they emit changes when it comes into contact with the energy of each chakra. This variation indicates the vibrational state of the chakras.

Naturally, you will need to have spent sufficient time working with your bowl to perceive when it emits a harmonious or distorted sound, dull or bright. Remember that the sound should always be clear and pure.

Once you have completed your personal practice and integrated all the information related to your bowls, you can begin working therapeutically with other people.

General harmonization technique

This therapy is performed standing, striking the bowl a minimum of three times and always waiting after each strike for the sound and vibration to cease. We will then proceed in the following order: Before beginning the session, we will briefly explain to our client what the therapy will entail.

- We will position our clients with their legs open approximately shoulder-width apart.

- We will ask them to close their eyes and take three deep breaths.

- We will place the bowl between their legs and strike it one to three times.

- We will wait for the sound to completely disappear before striking it again.

- Next, we will hold the bowl in our hands and strike it in front of the client at knee level.

- Then, we will strike the area of the first chakra.

- Finally, we will repeat the process around the fourth or heart chakra..

- With the final activation in the heart area, move the bowl above the head without striking it, until reaching the back of the fourth chakra. Activate it there three times.

- Move down to the coccyx area and activate the bowl three times.

- Continue down to the area behind the knees (the popliteal fossae) and strike the bowl three times.

- Finish by placing the bowl between the feet and activating it three times, in order to anchor the new energy that has been mobilized in the client.

If you wish to carry out a more complete harmonization and have enough time, you can also activate the bowl along the sides of the body.

- Begin at the feet, striking the bowl three times.

- Activate the bowl again at the level of the knees and the coccyx (three times).

- Repeat the process in the heart area and move over the head to the other side without striking.

- Return to the heart area and repeat the process, as well as around the first chakra, passing through the knees and finishing at the feet.

- End the harmonization session by placing the bowl between the feet and striking it three times to anchor the new energy transformed through the sound of the bowls.

To complete the session, allow the client a few minutes of silence and then offer a glass of water.

This harmonization can also be applied after other therapies such as Bach flower remedies, reflexology, or acupuncture. In such cases, the bowl will be activated only once at each point.

Chakra balancing

This therapy helps us balance and harmonize the energy of the chakras or to provide more specific treatment for a particular ailment. In the latter case, we will add another point of sound activation.

For example, if our client suffers from a lung condition, we will add activation of the lung area to the general healing by placing our singing bowl over that area and activating it at least three times.

115

Below, we explain step by step how to perform this healing.

Before beginning the session, we will briefly explain to our client what the therapy entails.

- Place the client lying face down on the treatment table.

- Ask them to close their eyes and take three deep breaths.

- Elevate the feet with a cushion or rolled towel and place the bowl on top, allowing you to better control its weight and sound. The bowl must be free to vibrate. You may place a rubber mat underneath the bowl to ensure stability.

- Focus yourself, then gently touch the area where you are going to place the bowl to inform the client and allow the gesture to be better received.

- First place the rubber mat on the soles of the feet, then the bowl. If it feels unstable, you may use your fingers as wedges, always ensuring that the rim of the bowl remains free to vibrate easily.

- Begin by striking the bowl three times in an ascending direction at the feet, allowing the sound to fully fade before striking again.

- You may set the intention of guiding the energy of the bowl upward toward the head, releasing whatever is blocked.

- Move the bowl to the knees and activate it three times.

- Then activate the root chakra. Hold the bowl with your hand without resting it on the client, as this is a sensitive and intimate area. Activate it approximately 15 centimeters above the chakra, three times.

- At the navel chakra, from this point onward, the bowl may rest on the client's body and be activated three times.

- At the solar plexus chakra.

- At the heart chakra.

- At the throat chakra. From this point on, hold the bowl without resting it on the client, as it can be uncomfortable and is an unstable and sensitive area close to the auditory system.

- At the third eye chakra. Holding it in your hand, activate it at a distance of 15 centimeters to avoid discomfort in the auditory area due to excessive sound and vibration.

- At the crown chakra, also activate it at a distance of 15 centimeters.

- Next, activate the specific point where your client's ailment is located. It is important to activate the bowl several times until its sound is pure, but if this is not achieved, it is advisable not to exceed twelve activations per point, as this could saturate or block the energy due to over-activation.

- Then, make your way back to the feet, striking the bowl downwards with the intention of anchoring the new and pure energy.

Once the session is finished, allow the person to return to their own pace, respecting a period of silence. Afterward, offer them a glass of water.

Energy Balancing

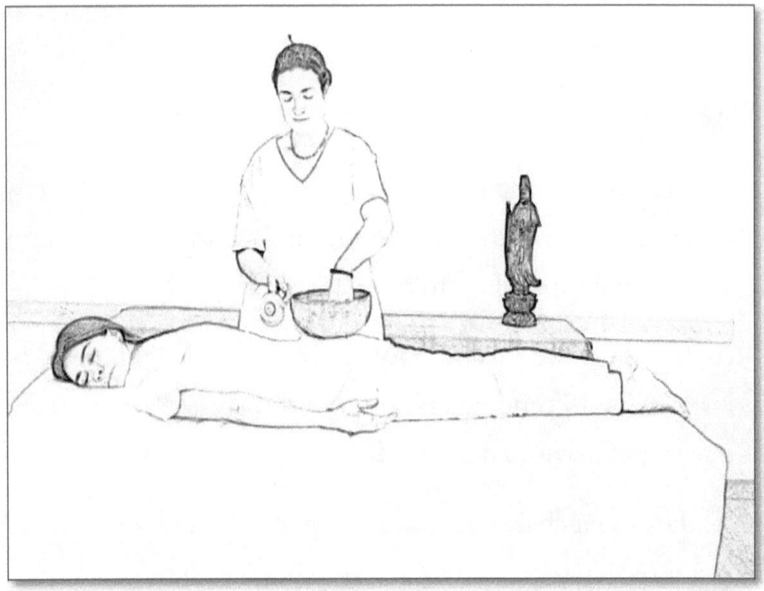

For this therapy, we will need a large singing bowl, a cotton mallet, and a leather-covered mallet.

This healing primarily works in the electromagnetic field and helps to release energy blockages that are affecting the physical body. We can address stress, an emotional and electromagnetic imbalance that, when prolonged, leads to physical problems such as chronic fatigue.

Steps to follow:

- Before beginning the session, we will briefly explain the therapy to our client.

- We will position our client lying face up on the treatment table or futon.

- If necessary, we will place cushions under the knees, lower back, and head to ensure maximum comfort and relaxation.

- We will ask the client to close their eyes and take three deep breaths.

- We will begin by activating the singing bowl about 20 centimeters (8 inches) from the client's feet. We will activate it only once, and before moving to a different area, we will wait for its sound to completely fade.

- Then, moving clockwise around the client, we will activate the bowl 20 centimeters from the knee area.

- Next, we will activate the root chakra 20 centimeters away, and so on, 20 cm around each chakra (sacral, solar plexus, heart, throat, third eye, and crown).

- From the crown chakra, we will follow the same steps, but on the opposite side, until we reach the feet.

- We will continue clockwise towards the feet, activating the bowl at the sixth, fifth, fourth, third, second, and first chakras, and at the knees, 20 centimeters from the feet.

- To finish, we will activate the bowl while moving from head to toe and back down, repeating this process three times. We will activate the bowl as many times as needed during this movement.

Once the healing session is over, allow the person to return to their own pace, respecting a period of silence. Afterwards, offer them a glass of water.

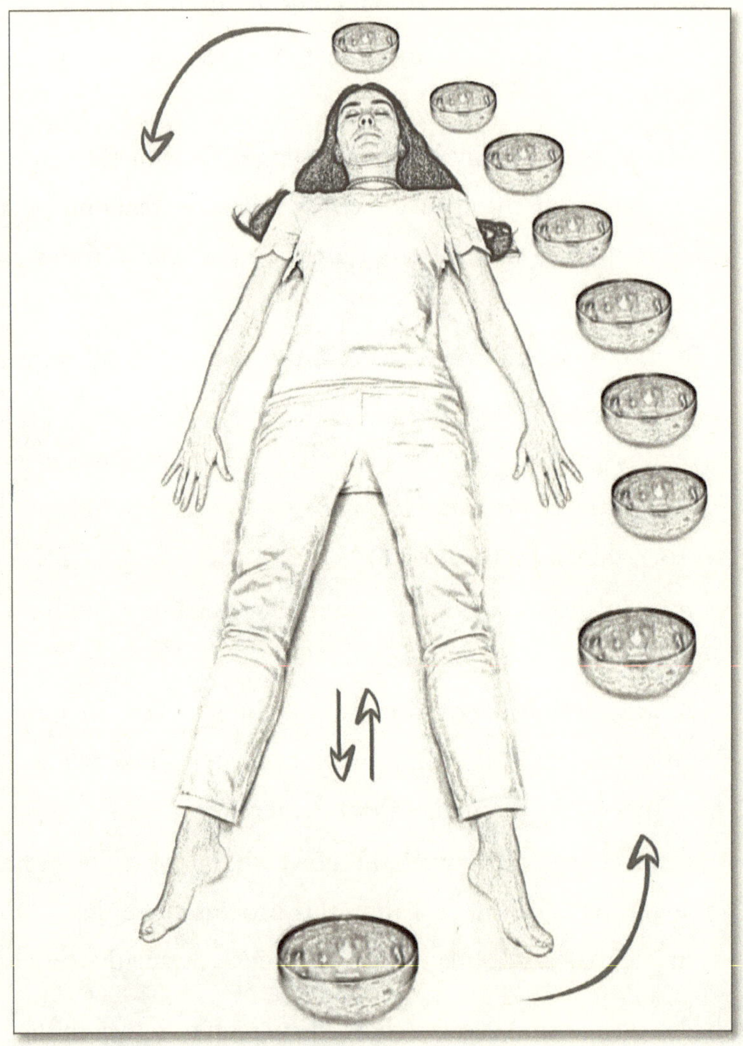

We can also activate and energize stones or crystals, Bach flower remedies, food, or water by passing the sound of the bowl around them. We can also accompany a person in their final moments of life or during childbirth, helping both processes unfold in a more harmonious way.

Ultimately, we can use this wonderful tool both to heal others and to benefit ourselves from the healing and balancing power it can bring into our lives.

6.15 Case Study

Daisy, a sixty-one-year-old civil servant, came to the consultation due to hip stiffness that prevented her from carrying out the normal tasks of daily life. She had been undergoing osteopathic treatment for two years without experiencing any improvement.

She read one of our articles about the benefits of sound therapy and decided she had nothing to lose by trying a session.

We agreed that the most suitable sound tool for her condition would be Tibetan singing bowls.

She lay down on the treatment table, and we applied the zonal tonal harmonization technique. During the process, Daisy began to experience muscular relaxation in her legs, which she described as "liberating." We worked with ascending activation up to the seventh chakra and then carried out a deep activation of both hips by placing the bowl on the iliac crests.

During the healing, she asked to work on the heart area, as she felt the need to release "something" she could not identify. During this process, she realized that her hip problem was caused by the cold and rigid relationship she had with her father. She cried intensely but emphasized that we should not stop playing the bowl while she cried, as it gave her great relief.

Once she felt she had released her burden, she told us we could continue with the session.

We ended the session and she thanked us for respecting her timing and her requests. She felt genuinely cared for.

We agreed that she would contact us again when she felt the moment was right, yet she asked for another appointment the following week. In that session, she told us she had visited her osteopath, who was very surprised by the change and said to her, literally: "What have you done? Your hip is aligned."

In this session, she asked to repeat the same technique as in the previous one, but this time focusing on the heart area in order to continue working on her relationship with her father.

During this session, she did not feel the need to cry, but many lived experiences with her father surfaced. Experiences she felt had long been hidden. We ended the session and she commented that she now felt able to face her relationship with her father with a sense of safety and without fear.

This case shows how important it is to listen and remain fully present in order to interpret the signals and wishes of our client, so that the therapy be as healing as possible.

CHAPTER 7

THE DRUM

Our bodies are rhythmic instruments, something we can observe in the process of breathing, which accelerates or slows down when we sleep, or in the rhythm of the heart, which becomes erratic during moments of physical or emotional stress.

In the mother's womb, our heart connects with our mother's heartbeat and later becomes an independent rhythm.

Rhythmic sounds connect us in a perceptible and direct way with our own body and also with the external world. Rhythm implies repetition; it is the foundation from which all sounds emerge.

Since ancient times, the drum has been one of the oldest and most universal instruments used by humankind for ritual, spiritual, and healing purposes. The earliest traces of its use date back to prehistoric cultures, where rhythm and sound were an essential part of community life, rites of passage, the relationship with nature, and the understanding of the invisible world.

Its presence is found in virtually every culture in the world. Indigenous peoples of Africa, the Americas, Asia, Oceania, and Europe have used the drum as a sacred tool, linked to the heartbeat of the earth, natural cycles, and group cohesion. In many of these cultures, the drum was not considered a mere musical instrument, but an object of power, laden with symbolism, representing the connection between heaven, earth, and humankind.

The sound of the drum is intimately linked to the rhythm of the heartbeat, the first sound we hear before birth in the womb. This primal pulse is imprinted on our body memory and explains why the drum feels so deeply familiar and comforting. Its vibration acts directly on the nervous system, helping to regulate internal rhythms, breathing, and emotional state.

The drum's repetitive pulse has traditionally been used to induce expanded states of consciousness, such as trance, active meditation, or deep relaxation. Through the steady rhythm, the rational mind quiets, facilitating access to deeper levels of perception, where the body activates its own self-regulating and healing mechanisms.

In many shamanic traditions, the drum has been used as a vehicle for inner journeys. The shaman or healer employed it to accompany visionary processes, soul retrieval, the release of emotional blocks, and energetic harmonization. The drum's sound set the pace of the journey, protected the ritual space, and sustained the therapeutic intention of the process.

In these contexts, the drum was not played as a conventional musical instrument, but as a ceremonial tool, always with a clear intention, prior preparation, and a deep respect for its vibrational power. Its use was closely linked to the healing of the individual, but also to the balance of the community and the relationship with the forces of nature.

Today, this ancestral knowledge is integrated and adapted to contemporary approaches to sound healing, reminding us that rhythm, vibration, and sound have accompanied humankind since its origins as universal languages of healing and connection.

The earliest evidence of the use of rhythm and the drum dates back more than 8,000 years, confirming its constant presence in the history of humanity. Numerous studies and texts document the varied uses of the drum within the pagan, spiritual, and religious practices of multiple cultures throughout time. Its applications have been as diverse as the people who have used it.

Each culture has developed its own rhythms, integrated into rituals and ceremonies that accompanied the most important moments of community life. The drum was present in annual celebrations such as planting and harvesting, in solar and lunar cycles—solstices and equinoxes—as well as in fundamental rites of passage such as birth, death, and marriage. It was also part of ritual dances, processions, healing ceremonies, and, in some contexts, activities related to hunting or warfare.

Beyond its ritual function, the sound of the drum played an essential role as an instrument of communication and spiritual transcendence. Its clear, deep, and penetrating sound allowed messages to be transmitted over great distances, across steppes, mountains, or jungles. These rhythms not only served as practical signals but also had symbolic meaning, connecting people with their environment, with the community, and with the sacred.

In this way, the drum became established as a universal language, capable of uniting the human and the spiritual, the individual and the collective, reminding us that rhythm and vibration have been, since the beginning, an essential form of communication, connection and healing.

7.1 The therapeutic effects of percussion

The sound of the drum is often described as "earthy," and it is true that many percussion enthusiasts experience a strong connection with Mother Earth. The intensity of the vibrations is transmitted throughout the body, activates circulation and lymphatic flow, and deepens breathing.

Playing percussion instruments with the hands regulates blood pressure, stimulates circulation, and massages reflex points in the fingers and palms, activating all the systems of the body.

Drum rhythms influence all bodily processes and brain impulses, allowing us to reach states conducive to meditation. In addition, they help release emotional blockages. Playing the drum or any percussion instrument allows us to express emotions and release stress.

This is why rhythm, dance, and singing come together in ceremonies: they help reduce worries and stimulate energy, making us feel happier and more balanced, and allowing us to fully enjoy the present moment.

According to recent studies, insecure, shy, or withdrawn individuals benefit the most from practicing percussion, as it encourages them to loosen inhibitions and express themselves freely, overcoming shame and insecurity.

The advantages of working with percussion are:

1. It transmits vibration throughout the body, activating it both physically and emotionally.

2. It stimulates circulation and deepens breathing.

3. It supports the body's natural rhythmic processes.

4. It releases tension and increases self-confidence.

5. It strengthens the first three chakras.

6. It connects us with the rhythms of nature.

7. It improves body awareness.

8. It stimulates passion and enjoyment of life.

9. It promotes self-healing.

10. It harmonizes the cerebral hemispheres.

11. It helps reduce stress and anxiety processes.

12. It helps eliminate toxins from the body.

13. It regulates heart rhythm.

14. It stabilizes sleep rhythms.

7.2 Percussion for chakra harmony

Rhythmic elements are closely related to the first three chakras. If we pay attention, we notice that when we hear drum sounds, the vibration is felt mainly from the feet up to the upper abdomen.

The Muladhara chakra represents vital energy—our survival connected to the Earth and nature. When the energy flow of this chakra is blocked, we experience lack of energy and insecurity.

Practice of percussion is perhaps the most appropriate and recommended technique to balance the root chakra. This practice provides strength, confidence, and a sense of security.

The sound of the drum also harmonizes with the second chakra, Svadhisthana, activating our sexual energy and creative spirit. Percussion stimulates eroticism, passion, and vitality.

In the case of the third chakra, Manipura, percussion provides the energy needed to project ourselves into the world and develop the personal power required to achieve our goals. As a result, when these first three chakras are balanced and harmonized, all the others are deeply supported and strengthened, producing an overall balance of the energetic system.

7.3 Percussion and the brain

To date, there is only a limited amount of scientific research on the physiological and neurological effects of drumming, which can be summarized as follows:

1. **Loss of temporal continuum (LTC):** several participants reported losing their sense of time during percussion sessions.

2. **Sensations of bodily vibration:** feelings of parts of the body vibrating or expanding, pressure on the body or specific areas, waves of energy moving through the body, sensations of flying or spiraling.

3. **Energization:** participants specifically mentioned feeling more energized during or after the percussion session.

4. **Temperature fluctuations:** some experienced unexpected changes in temperature, chills, warmth, or sweating.

5. **Relaxation and mental clarity:** most participants reported feeling deeply relaxed and mentally alert.

6. **Out-of-body experiences:** some experienced leaving the room while their body remained in it.

7. **Perception of entities:** during the session, some felt the presence of incorporeal beings, such as animals or deceased individuals known to them.

8. **Visual imagery:** participants reported seeing colors, images, and geometric shapes.

Native Americans refer to the sound of the drum as "the heartbeat of the Earth." The frequency of the Earth's electromagnetic resonance, measured at approximately 7.5 cycles per second, corresponds to theta brain waves. For this reason, the sound of the drum allows shamans to align their brain waves with the vibration of the Earth.

In China, archaeological research has discovered cave paintings related to the rhythms of the I Ching, represented in the Bagua, which is composed of eight trigrams. According to Taoist philosophy, it is possible to apply drum rhythms to the I Ching.

The I Ching, or *Book of Changes*, is an ancient Chinese book of wisdom consisting of sixty-four hexagrams, each related to aspects of archetypal or universal energies.

Each hexagram contains six lines; these lines are either continuous (—)
or broken (- -). Continuous lines represent a complete drumbeat, and
broken lines represent two rhythmic pulses.

Research conducted using electroencephalograms has confirmed that
percussion practices produce changes in the brain's electrical activity,
increasing the presence of alpha rhythms, associated with meditative
states, and theta rhythms, which are linked to the first stages of sleep.

7.4 Percussion and Trance

Nevill Drury, in his book *The Elements of Shamanism*, writes:

*"There is something that never ceases to amaze me: after approximately one hour of
drumming, ordinary city people are capable of connecting with extraordinary mystical
realities they had never imagined."*

To journey into the subconscious, the shaman enters a specific altered
state of consciousness that requires remaining alert and aware. In this
state, the shaman can move at will between different dimensions.

Michael Harner referred to this as the Shamanic State of Consciousness (SSC):

"There are several techniques for entering the SSC, including sensory deprivation, fasting, hyperventilation, dancing, chanting or recitation, drumming, exposure to extreme temperatures, and the use of ritual settings prescribed by cultural beliefs and ceremonies. However, the sound of monotonous rhythms is the fastest path to trance states. This is why, throughout the world, the drum remains the preferred instrument of healers. The trance induced by these rhythms activates healing processes and supports bodily regeneration."

Other researchers, such as the anthropologist R. Needham, raised similar questions:

"The most common description found repeatedly in ethnographic literature states that the shaman drums to establish contact with spirits," and *"it has been observed worldwide that percussion, in whatever form it takes, enables and accompanies communication with the other world."*

There are many theories regarding this phenomenon, but no scientific explanation has yet been found.

Shamans explain that to initiate the "journey into the subconscious," it is necessary to engage in rhythmic drumming sessions, as these facilitate entry into altered states of consciousness. To promote a mental state conducive to this journey, it is necessary to listen to a rhythmic sound of 205 to 220 beats per minute. This rhythm prompts the brain to produce slow brain waves, from 7 to 4 cycles per second or less.

Additionally, the sound of the drum is described as "the voice of the spirits." It is said that the shaman makes the drum frame from a piece of the Tree of Life provided by spiritual guides. Thus, each time the shaman plays the drum, they connect with the center of Mother Earth and establish a personal relationship with the drum.

Shamans and healers from Siberia and the Middle East use flat drums with two skins, allowing them to be played on both sides. In North America, healers descended from Native American traditions use larger drums.

7.5 Types of therapeutic drums and their uses

Throughout different cultures and traditions, the drum has taken on distinct forms and functions depending on the ritual context, the natural environment, and the therapeutic purpose. Currently, some of these drums are commonly used in sound healing and emotional support.

Shamanic Drum

The shamanic drum is one of the best known and most widely used in ancestral healing contexts. It is generally constructed with a wooden hoop and stretched natural skin and is played with a soft mallet.

Its deep, repetitive sound facilitates states of inner journeying, light trance, and connection with the unconscious. It is especially used to:

- Promote grounding and connection with the earth
- Support processes of introspection and self-knowledge
- Release deep emotional blocks
- Recover vital energy in moments of exhaustion
- Work on symbolic processes of healing and transformation

It is a very powerful drum energetically, so it is recommended to use it with a clear intention and in well-contained sessions.

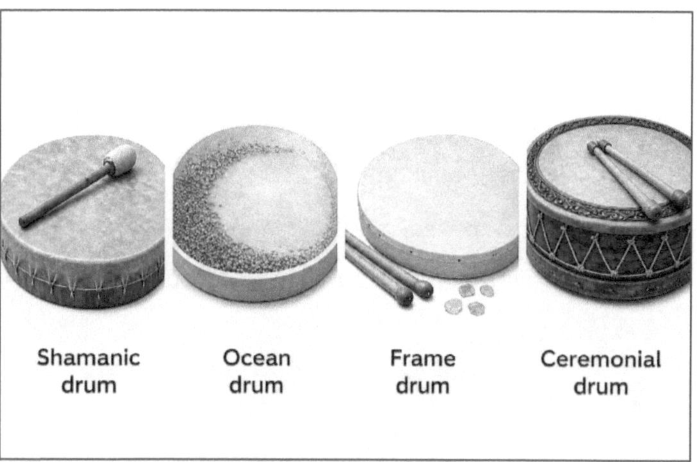

Ocean Drum

The ocean drum contains small beads or seeds inside which, when moved, generate a sound like that of the sea and waves. Its vibration is soft, enveloping, and deeply relaxing, making it an ideal instrument for:

- Inducing states of deep relaxation

- Supporting processes of anxiety and stress

- Facilitating rest and sleep

- Working with children, sensitive individuals, or those with high emotional stress

- Acting especially on the nervous system, providing a sense of calm, containment, and security.

Frame Drum

The frame drum is a large drum with a broad sound, used in many Mediterranean, Eastern, and shamanic cultures. It is used to:

- Work on body rhythm and coordination
- Encourage emotional expression through movement
- Gradually activate vital energy
- Accompany group work and ceremonies
- Its sound is less deep than the shamanic drum, but more versatile and expressive.

Ritual or Ceremonial Drum

Some drums are specifically designed for rituals, ceremonies, and collective celebrations. Their main function is to generate group cohesion, establish a common rhythm, and create a shared vibrational field.

They are used to:

- Strengthening the sense of belonging
- Accompany rites of passage
- Raise group energy
- Create states of collective connection

7.6 Other percussion instruments for healing

Tuned percussion instruments

These are percussion instruments that can produce various notes; that is, they are melodic because they can play different melodies. Examples include the xylophone, marimba, vibraphone, glockenspiel, timpani, etc.

All of these require mallets to be played, just like untuned instruments. These instruments could be used in healing, but their size makes them difficult to use. They can be used in group therapy sessions of eight or more people, which is very interesting because it combines rhythmic percussion with harmonic melodies.

Untuned percussion instruments

These instruments are known as pitch-indeterminate percussion instruments. They are percussion instruments whose sound does not produce a specific or defined note; that is, they cannot produce different pitches. For this reason, it is not possible to play melodies or musical scales with them, since their main function is rhythmic and vibrational, rather than melodic.

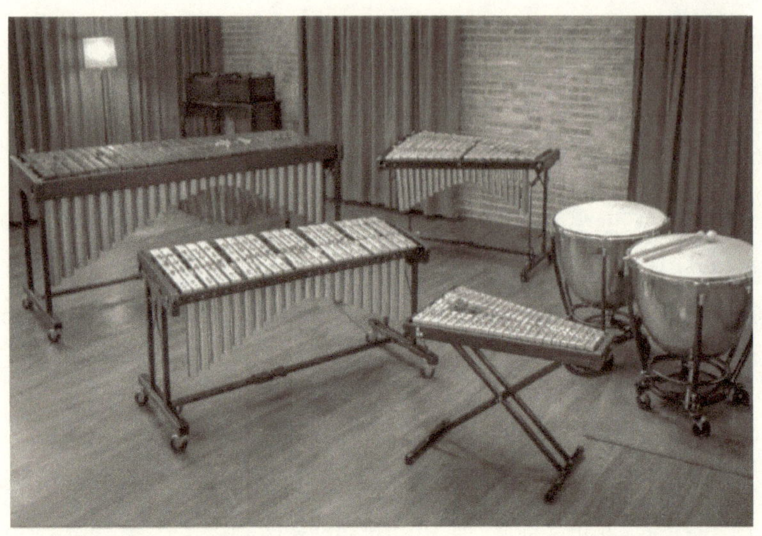

Despite not being tuned to a specific frequency, these instruments have great value in sound healing and therapeutic work. Their sound, generally low, deep, or dry, acts directly on the body through vibration, promoting the release of tension, the regulation of internal rhythm, and connection with the body's pulse.

Among the best-known pitch indeterminate percussion instruments are the drum, bass drum, cymbals, triangle, castanets, claves, shaker, maracas, cajón, and various types of rattles and drumheads. Each of these instruments contributes a distinct sound quality, which can be used for therapeutic purposes depending on the session's objective.

In sound healing, these instruments are primarily used to work on rhythm, grounding, emotional release, and the activation of bodily energy. Thanks to their size and the controllable intensity of their sound, they can be used safely in both individual and group sessions, adapting to each person's needs.

Although they do not generate melody, their ability to organize internal rhythm and stimulate bodily responses makes them highly effective tools within therapeutic support processes, helping to restore physical, emotional, and energetic balance.

7.7 Find your drum

For your rhythmic healing sessions, we recommend using a shamanic drum, due to its healing power.

Our recommendations are:

- The drumheads should be made of animal skin, as plastic or tin emits a very loud and unpleasant sound, and the vibration they produce does not have a healing function.
- The drumhead should be taught and firmly attached to the drum body.

- Its size should be appropriate for the size of your hand, so you can hold it firmly and easily play it.

- First, touch the drum with your hands and observe what it makes you feel, to create an interaction with the drum and begin to perceive its sound.

- Activate the drum with your hands and different drumsticks to obtain the full range of sounds and vibrations that this particular instrument can produce.

- Take the time you need to observe, play, and listen to the different models.

When you feel a special connection with one of them, congratulations, you have found your drum!

7.8 Drum care

Like all instruments, the drum requires proper care to maintain sound quality:

- Do not expose it to sudden temperature changes, as the drumhead may lose tension.

- Never wash it with water or detergent.

- When not in use, store it in a protective case to prevent impacts and extreme temperatures.

- Never place objects on the drumhead.

- If the drumhead is synthetic, do not oil it; if it is natural skin, follow the manufacturer's care instructions.

- Do not rest the drum on the surface with the skin facing down.

- If playing with your hands, avoid wearing rings that could scratch the drumhead.

7.9 Exercise to activate your inner rhythm

Next, we'll explore several rhythmic exercises that require no prior experience. However, it's important to dedicate time to them, in a quiet place where you won't be disturbed, so you can experience and integrate the healing power of rhythm.

Find your own rhythm

For this exercise, you can sit or lie on your back. Choose a position that allows you to relax and close your eyes. If any thoughts arise, don't worry about them; simply let them go.

- When you're ready, place a hand on your heart and listen to its rhythm… take some time to connect with your own rhythm, focusing your attention on the interval between each beat.

- When you feel you've identified your heart's rhythm, let's reproduce it with your hands, clapping to the same rhythm as your heartbeat. Do the same by tapping a drum or gently tapping your legs, chest, or arms. •

- Once you've internalized your heart rate, try adding two pulses (or two claps) between each heartbeat. Once you've perfected this, practice adding three or four pulses per beat.

- After experiencing these rhythms, introduce the pauses: pulse, pause, pulse, pause… and so on.

The following exercise can be done with any type of percussion instrument, in a group or individually.

Percussive gale

This exercise consists of gradually increasing the intensity of the drum's sound until you create a sonic gale.

- Sit relaxed on the floor or a chair and pick up your favorite percussion instrument. Start playing softly, so that the sound is barely audible. You don't need to follow a specific rhythm. Close your eyes and let your breath flow freely and the sound gradually increases.
- Gradually increases the intensity until the instrument emits a thunderous sound. Once you've reached the peak, begin to decrease the instrument's intensity, as if the sounds were fading into the distance, slowly dying away.

In this practice, you may experience physiological changes as you increase the intensity. For example, your temperature will rise, your heart rate will increase, and your breathing will accelerate.

Conversely, when you decrease the intensity, you'll notice how you become calmer, your muscles relax, and your heart rate slows…

7.10 Healing techniques with percussion

Energizing the chakras

In this therapy we will work on harmonizing and enhancing the correct flow of energy through the chakras.

- First, the client lies on their back, and we take our shamanic drum, positioning ourselves about 20 centimeters from their feet.

- We begin activating the drum with soft, continuous beats. Gradually, we increase the intensity and rhythm until reaching the drum's maximum volume.

- Once this point is reached, we slowly decrease the intensity until it almost disappears. This process should last approximately two minutes.

- After the first activation, we move to the knee area and repeat the same steps.

- Next, we repeat this process at the level of the first, second, third, fourth, fifth, sixth, and seventh chakras, and finally 20 centimeters from the client's head.

- Then, if possible, we ask the client to turn face down, and we continue the therapy.

- In this position, we begin activating the drum, as previously described, 20 centimeters from the head, and then descend in the following order:
20 centimeters from the head, seventh, sixth, fifth, fourth, third, second, and first chakras, knee area, foot area, and finally 20 centimeters beyond the feet.

Once the therapy is completed, we allow a few minutes of silence and prepare a glass of water to help the client return to a state of presence.

A variation for addressing specific areas of discomfort:

If the client is experiencing a particular ailment, we can perform a gentle rhythmic activation for five to ten minutes.

First, the client will lie on their back. We will then take our shamanic drum, position ourselves about 20 centimeters from their feet, and begin activating the drum with gentle, continuous strokes for about two minutes.

- Next, we perform the steps described in the "Energizing the Chakras" technique, with one difference: we ascend through the feet, knees, and chakras, maintaining activation for only one minute at each point.

- Once the chakras have been activated and we reach the head area, we then treat the specific area or areas affected by the client.

- To do this, we place the drum about 20 centimeters away, directing the center of the drumhead toward the specific area, and activate the drum for a minimum of six minutes.

- Care should be taken to ensure the sound is not uncomfortable. If it is, we should move slightly farther away until the client feels comfortable.

- Once the localized treatment is finished, we position ourselves at the head and descend through the chakras to the feet, maintaining activation for one minute at each point.

At the end of the session, we again allow a few minutes of silence and offer a glass of water to help the client fully return to presence.

Aura Protection

To perform this, we need a large drum that emits the deepest and most resonant sound possible, such as a shamanic drum or a Celtic tambourine. The drum's sounds can be used directly to strengthen the aura and activate our "psychic defenses." To do this, we will proceed as follows:

- We will have the client stand, ask them to half-close their eyes, without ever closing them completely, fixing their gaze on an undefined point, and relaxing by concentrating on their breathing.

- The therapist begins to build a protective aura by gently striking the drumhead with their hands or a mallet. The important thing is to create a continuous, rapid, clear, yet delicate sound.

- While performing the exercise, the drum should be about a meter away, although the recommended distance may vary depending on several factors, such as the force of the strike or the client's sensitivity.

- The therapist stands facing the client, at foot level, and strikes the drum three times continuously, moving up to the calves and then to the knees.

- Once the feet and knees are filled with the sound of the drum, the therapist continues upward, moving from the pubic area to the navel, chest, throat, and between the eyebrows, until reaching the head.

- Next, the therapist places the drum at the crown of the client's head, always at a safe distance from the ear, and begins to move down the back of the client's body, continuing to strike the drum.

- The vibrations of the drum will then surround the neck, shoulder blades, kidneys, buttocks, calves, and feet.

Once the therapy is complete, the client should take some time to feel the effects. In addition to strengthening the aura, the vibrations activate the respiratory system, deepening the breath and purifying and strengthening the chakras.

7.11 Case Study

William, a twenty-one-year-old student, came to therapy after failing his driving test three times. He needed to pass because he felt like a failure.

In his own words, his anxiety and fear of failing again were so intense that his hands sweated so much he could barely hold the steering wheel, and his legs trembled uncontrollably.

We agreed that the most appropriate therapy to help him manage his fear and anxiety was to work with the shamanic drum, focusing on the first chakra, to balance fear and strengthen his sense of safety.

William lay down, and we began the technique "Healing Specific Points." We ascended from the feet to the head, activating the drum for one minute at each point. Once this first process was completed, we activated the first chakra for six minutes. However, after this time we noticed that his breathing had become faster and that the tension was concentrated in the stomach area.

We decided to activate the solar plexus chakra to rebalance his breathing, reduce anxiety, and mobilize his personal power. He needed this support to strengthen his self-esteem and pass the exam.

We began activating this chakra, but after six minutes his breathing had not yet relaxed sufficiently, so I chose to continue for a few more minutes. Once his breathing became harmonious again, we continued the technique, descending from the head down to the feet.

At the end of the session William felt lighter and more relaxed. He even noticed that his body felt less heavy. When we asked him how he felt when thinking about the exam, he confirmed that he felt much more confident.

William o returned three days later to reinforce this sense of safety and self-confidence, and we repeated the same technique used in the previous session.

The following week, I received a call from William to thank us for the help, as he had finally passed his driving test.

CHAPTER 8

QUARTZ CRYSTAL BOWLS

Quartz crystal bowls are based on the tradition of using Tibetan bowls and bring a new dimension to the world of vibration and sound.

When you listen to and feel the sound and vibration of quartz bowls, every cell in your body receives a vibrational massage that relaxes you, producing a deep state of physical, emotional, mental, and energetic well-being.

The sound vibrations of these bowls help us restructure our molecules, improve the connection between our brain frequencies, strengthen our electromagnetic field or aura, and enhance our emotional state.

The origin of quartz bowls is relatively recent. They emerged in the 1980s, when experimentation began with quartz powder and its fusion.

To better understand this process, let us look at the different stages quartz must go through to become a bowl:

1. **Quartz crushing.** First, the quartz is crushed into pieces approximately 7.5 centimeters in diameter. In the second stage, it is ground down to about 2.5 centimeters, producing silica powder.

2. **Fusion in an electric furnace.** The silica powder is packed as tightly as possible into a graphite or carbon mold to prevent small amounts of air from entering, which could create bubbles and cause the bowl to crack.

    These molds are placed in a vacuum furnace at a temperature of 4,000°C, where the quartz is fused.

3. **Compacting and polishing.** The manufacturing process is complex. In this final stage, the bowls are polished and any possible imperfections are removed using specialized machinery.

8.1 Characteristics of quartz crystal bowls

Quartz is one of the most abundant minerals on the planet and has a strong resonance with human beings, as crystalline substances are present in our bodies—in our bones, blood, hair, skin, nails, and more.

In addition, our DNA has a double-helix structure very similar to that of quartz crystal. We also have four silica molecules per cell, and silica is present in the liquid crystalline–colloidal structure of the brain. All of this creates a strong resonance between humans and crystals.

Quartz acts as a conductor and transformer of energy. It has the quality of being *acoustic-luminescent*, meaning it can convert sound waves into light. In the technological industry, it is widely used due to its *piezoelectric* properties, which allow it to transmit information from one place to another.

Quartz crystals vibrate in a regular manner and have an internal spiral molecular structure. This causes quartz bowls to produce a pure sinusoidal wave, creating a multidirectional sound that can expand up to one kilometer and take several minutes to fade away.

8.2 The healing effects of quartz crystal bowls

The vibrations produced by the bowls surround us and create a state of relaxation that allows us to activate our healing energy, while leading us into a deep state of well-being.

However, their vibrations are so powerful that when some people are exposed to these frequencies, they may feel restless, nervous, or experience physical discomfort such as headaches, nausea, or dizziness.

This happens because the sound of the bowls acts like a *scalpel*, stirring stagnant emotional and mental states and triggering a healing crisis that will give way to a new order once the coherent frequencies emitted by the bowls are integrated into our systems.

Each person needs their own time to integrate the changes produced by these frequencies. Their speed and intensity can be so powerful that, at times, they do not allow enough space for the person to process the change calmly and harmoniously, which can lead to more or less intense healing crises.

For this reason, it is essential to pay close attention to each client's needs—observing when it is appropriate to use certain frequencies and determining the appropriate duration of exposure. Otherwise, overstimulation may occur, leading to an acute healing crisis.

From our experience, it is quite common to see people leave a quartz bowl concert after a short time. This is not because the therapist lacks experience or because the sounds are harmful, but because, as mentioned above, the sounds of the bowls stir deeply held emotional and mental processes, and not everyone is at the right moment to handle the changes this may bring.

We advise these people not to stop exploring the benefits of these sounds, but to gradually become accustomed to them, slowly increasing their exposure time as they begin to feel more comfortable.

However, it is not advisable to exceed **50 minutes**, as after this time the body has already integrated the frequencies it needs and may become overstimulated, producing a feeling of lethargy. As with everything in life, balance lies in moderation.

It is also important to know that even if people fall asleep during a session or concert, the healing effects of these bowl frequencies continue to work on them.

Its healing power is so remarkable that Dr. Gaynor uses the sound and vibrations of these instruments to help his clients with life-threatening or chronic illnesses. He also says:

"Sound can guide us, like a laser, to the very center of our essence, to the highest realization of a healthy spirit and body."

On a more general level, we can highlight other properties of quartz crystal singing bowl therapy:

- Balances the auric field.

- The sound of the bowls allows one to travel through altered states of consciousness, as its influence modifies brain waves.

- Balances the nervous system.

- Promotes blood circulation.

- Promotes cellular oxygenation.

- Modifies adrenaline levels.

- Improves breathing rhythm.

- Provides a gentle massage to our internal organs.

- Releases tension and emotional blockages.

- Provides security and confidence.

- Harmonizes the brain hemispheres.

- Releases muscle tension.

- It is helpful for bone problems.

- It effectively treats osteoarthritis.

- It dissolves kidney stones.

- It is very effective for depression.

- It stimulates neuronal connections.

- It is effective in cases of Alzheimer's disease.

- It corrects dyslexia and ADHD.

- It enhances flower essences and essential oils.

If we fill a bowl with water and turn on its sound, we can observe how geometric shapes form within the water. If we try to increase the intensity, we will see how the water begins to fizz.

This can give us an idea of the effect these instruments have on the body, which is composed of more than 70 percent water. In this regard, Dr.

Jeffrey Thompson, director of the Center for Neuroacoustic Research at the California Institute of Human Sciences, says:

"Since sound travels five times better through water than through air, stimulating the body with sound frequencies is a very effective form of whole-body stimulation, especially at the cellular level."

Direct stimulation of living cellular tissue, using sound frequency vibrations, enhances cellular metabolism, thereby enabling the mobilization of a cellular healing response.

The sound of these bowls affects the person holistically, balancing the energy body, chakras, nadis, and auric field.

Depending on their size, the frequencies to which they are tuned, and the crystals from which the bowls are made, they will be used to address the different ailments that clients may present during therapy.

The low sounds, from bowls with a diameter between 40 and 60 centimeters, are used to balance, harmonize, and ground the first three chakras due to their deep, resonant, and expansive tones.

The higher sounds, from bowls between 18 and 35 centimeters, resonate with the upper chakras because of their more focused, sharp, and penetrating tones.

8.3 Types of crystal bowls

Since these instruments began to be used therapeutically, new combinations of crystals and minerals have been studied and developed. The most well-known types include:

- **Frosted**: White, opaque, and very solid; sizes range from 15 to 60 cm.

- **Clear**: Transparent, polished, and delicate; sizes range from 13 to 20 cm.

- **Colored**: Quartz varieties such as rose quartz, smoky quartz, and rutilated quartz; sizes range from 18 to 23 cm.

- **Alchemical**: The result of blending quartz crystal with different minerals and metals; available in various diameters.

For therapeutic use, some bowls are made with a small handle. These bowls are generally smaller, with diameters between 14 and 18 cm, to avoid excessive weight and to facilitate movement around the client's body.

8.4 Alchemical varieties

In general, higher-pitched sounds come from smaller bowls, while deeper tones come from bowls with a larger diameter. Sound also varies depending on wall thickness, and in alchemical bowls, it changes according to the minerals fused into the quartz.

Classic Gold

This bowl is coated with 24-karat gold. It develops energy related to action, success, and nobility, expanding the soul. It reconnects you with your higher self, energizes the body at a molecular level, and helps you understand and integrate life experiences.

Water Gold

This bowl helps balance the analytical mind and transform emotional blockages that cause disharmony. It cleanses and activates the upper chakras. Its masculine energy and color help relieve depression and lift the spirit.

Ocean Gold

This bowl encourages communication and activates the thymus gland and the throat chakra. The masculine frequencies of gold combined with water elements generate love, balance, self-realization, and adaptation to nature's healing forces.

White Gold

The pure frequencies of this bowl enhance imagination, creativity, and connection with the inner child. It also works powerfully with the solar plexus, strengthening self-esteem, artistic expression, and prosperity.

This blend of white gold and quartz crystal creates gentle, subtle, high-vibration frequencies that support self-confidence.

Platinum

The platinum bowl stimulates feminine energy, relieves stress and depression, aligns the emotional body, and develops intuition. It unifies the physical and emotional bodies, has a calming effect, and provides grounding and structure, fostering inner connection.

Mother-of-Pearl

A natural harmonizer combining quartz crystal with pearl essence, transmitting the energy of Venus, the goddess of love.

Pearl energy represents the constant presence and fullness of spirit. It helps work through emotional issues and develop nurturing qualities within a safe, comforting space.

Rose Quartz

This bowl is a fusion of natural rose quartz and clear quartz crystal. The calming and healing qualities of rose quartz are well known.

Its natural affinity with love makes it a wonderful tool for the heart chakra.

Its vibrational energies flow gently through the auric fields, helping to release emotional trauma, dissolve blockages, and restore a natural state of happiness.

Moldavite

This bowl is created through a special process that fuses moldavite into the crystalline structure of the bowl, altering its tonal structure and producing a truly otherworldly sound. This unique bowl deeply impacts anyone who sees or hears it.

Moldavite is a meteorite-impacted stone whose high-frequency energy catalyzes change, supports growth and transformation, opens the heart, and enhances connection with universal energy.

It develops psychic perception, expands mental awareness, supports meditation, and aligns the being with Higher Purpose.

Amethyst

This bowl enhances spiritual growth and supports the expansion of the third-eye chakra, fostering intuition and wisdom.

Amethysts help with personal transformation and understanding the lessons and opportunities behind moments of crisis and life challenges. It evokes serenity and intuitive clarity, helping balance mind and body.

Ruby

This bowl unites the loving protection of ruby with quartz crystal, radiating spiritual wisdom, health, and abundance. With its reddish tones, the ruby bowl strengthens self-confidence, survival instincts, and the ability to generate financial resources.

Citrine

A member of the quartz family, Citrine aligns the root and solar plexus chakras. Known as the legendary "merchant's stone," it helps expand and sustain prosperity.

The citrine bowl enhances optimism, balance, initiative, and personal power, while also strengthening self-esteem.

Great Mother

The love and nurturing care of the Earth's ancestral energy are represented in this bowl. Its vibration guides you toward connection with the timeless wisdom of the soul.

The fusion of quartz crystal and iron aligns you with strength, oxygenates the blood, energizes the entire body, and restores the desire to live.

Buddha

This new bowl is associated with joy, relaxation, letting go, creativity, prosperity, peace, and wisdom. The Buddha bowl radiates the love, compassion, and joviality of Eastern teachings.

Great Father

The essence of this bowl lies in the union of ancestral masculine wisdom with the energies of the Earth.

It helps us connect with our ancestral heritage in order to develop our virtues and inner knowledge. It inspires diplomacy and discernment rooted in traditional values.

Smoky Quartz

Smoky quartz promotes stability and balance. This bowl works with the root chakra, enhancing security and procreation.

Its serene energies encourage cooperation and a sense of belonging within the group.

Indium

This deep violet-blue bowl contains indium, a mineral that supports the absorption of vitamins and minerals and helps balance bodily energy alignment.

It illuminates inner life, giving access to all aspects of the Self. It supports physical change toward masculine/feminine balance and transcends cultural belief systems.

Ocean Indium

This bowl emits a high, gentle frequency that communicates with the body and helps it adapt to a state of balance.

Enhanced with indium, this trace element promotes longevity. It acts as a catalyst for improving lifestyle, increasing mobility, activating the third eye (pineal gland), and supporting spiritual alignment.

Egyptian Indigo

The Egyptian Indigo bowl is composed of vanadium, considered one of the oldest metals known, and is designed and created to harmoniously connect with ancient wisdom.

8.5 How to choose your crystal bowl

First, observe the bowls and notice whether one draws your attention particularly through its brightness, shape, color, or texture. Once you have chosen a bowl based on one of these qualities, place it in a safe position and follow these steps:

1. Place your hands on the upper rim, close your eyes, and observe how after a while you begin to feel vibration, tingling, or warmth in your hands. You may notice a sensation as if the circle was expanding.

2. Then you will feel the circle contract, accompanied by a slight sensation of cold. The energetic movement can be described as similar to a heartbeat.

3. Repeat the process, this time placing your hands around the bowl, and observe.

4. Finally, place your hands on the base of the bowl, making sure it does not fall, and prepare to experience the sensation.

8.6 How to connect with your crystal bowl

It is advisable to "tune in" to the bowls when we acquire them and before beginning to use them. This allows us to energetically align with their healing power.

The process follows these steps:

1. Place the bowl upside down and rest your hands on top of it.

2. Focus on the energy emitted by the bowl.

3. Knowing the note to which the bowl is tuned, focus on the color of the chakra it represents, with the intention of activating its energy so it can transmit it for healing purposes.

4. Turn the bowl upright and express your gratitude. Depending on your beliefs, you may invoke a spiritual guide, universal energy, or similar forces.

Another way to tune into the bowls is to place them upside down, activate a 528 Hz tuning fork, and place its tip on the base of the bowl.

Repeat this activation three times, then proceed with the gratitude phase described above.

When the therapist is experiencing or going through personal crises or deep internal changes, it is advisable to repeat this activation process to retune to the healing energy of the crystal bowl and be able to fully carry out healing sessions.

At times, a bowl may not sound as it should, and this can be due to several reasons:

- The person's energy is not compatible with the bowl. This may be temporary.
- The person activating the bowl is physically ill.
- The person is emotionally imbalanced.
- The ambient temperature is very low.
- The bowl only recognizes the energy of the person who uses it. For this reason, just as with minerals, they are not lent. Each person uses their own.

8.7 Ways to activate crystal bowls

To get the most out of the bowls, the most suitable place to position them is on the floor, especially if it is wooden, as it transmits the vibrations produced by these instruments very effectively.

For this reason, therapies, meditation, or concerts are carried out with people lying down, so they can experience and feel the vibrations coming through the floor.

Before activating the bowl, place it on a firm surface. On top of this, place a rubber ring to ensure complete stability and prevent the bowl from moving when activated and possibly breaking.

To activate medium and small frosted bowls and alchemical bowls, mallets are used that are usually made of plastic, leather-wrapped, or with wooden handles.

In the case of large, frosted bowls, wooden mallets with a rubber ball at the end are used to avoid the clicking sounds produced by friction, resulting in a softer and gentler sound.

There are three basic ways to activate them:

1. With a soft, slow strike on the upper part.

2. With gentle, rhythmic, and constant strikes on the upper part.

3. By rubbing the mallet around the outer rim, never inside, maintaining constant pressure.

Rubbing rotations can be either clockwise or counterclockwise.

Activate the bowl approximately 5 centimeters from the upper outer rim, whether striking or rubbing, and never activate it inside, as it could crack.

8.8 Cleaning and maintaining crystal bowls

Since the bowl contains living mineral material, minimal care is required to preserve its sound and vibration. It is advisable to keep the bowls hydrated to prevent them from cracking.

They can be hydrated using a spray bottle with distilled water.

Although bowls are cleaned by their own vibration, optionally the vibration of a 4,096 Hz angelic tuning fork can be applied to enhance this cleansing.

They can also be filled with water and placed in the sun for 20 minutes to hydrate them, then emptied and dried with a clean cloth.

The ideal storage for bowls is a special case lined with foam rubber or polystyrene to prevent possible knocks and to make transport easier.

They can also be placed on shelves as decorative objects. In this case, they should be cleaned and hydrated more frequently.

8.9 Exercise with crystal bowls

Before beginning to carry out the therapy with these wonderful instruments, it is necessary for us, as therapists, to perceive and experience their vibrations and sounds.

To help you with this, we offer several guided meditations, which you can find in the following QR code, accompanied by the sounds of crystal singing bowls.

You can also access the meditations in written format to read them, record your own voice, or use them in individual or group relaxation and healing sessions.

You can also access it from this link:

https://thewingbook.com/bonus/sound_therapy/

8.10 Healing techniques with crystal bowls

Healing with one crystal bowl

Sound therapy with crystal bowls is performed on the floor, as the sound of the bowls works best at the same level as the client.

The person lies on the floor, on a mat or blanket, and is covered with a white sheet or blanket.

We will ensure that the client is not wearing minerals, watches, metal objects, etc., so as not to interfere with the healing session. The therapist selects the bowl that will best aid the client's healing.

We will begin by activating the bowl as follows:

- First, we will activate the bowl about 20 centimeters (8 inches) from the client's feet for about three minutes. It is important to let the bowl finish sounding before moving on to harmonize the chakras.

- We will place the bowl on the left side, at the level of the first chakra, about 20 centimeters (8 inches) from the client. Activating it at least three times, and before moving on to another chakra, we will wait for its sound to completely fade.

- Next, we will repeat the same steps described above for each of the remaining chakras, in the sequential order of second, third, fourth, fifth, sixth, and seventh chakras. Once the seventh chakra is activated, we will move down the right side, harmonizing the sixth, fifth, fourth, third, second, and first chakras, finishing by harmonizing 20 centimeters from the feet.

- Then, we will move back up to harmonize the seventh chakra again and return to the starting point, 20 centimeters from the feet, to close and open the entire electromagnetic field.

We will conclude by offering water to our client to help them return to the present moment.

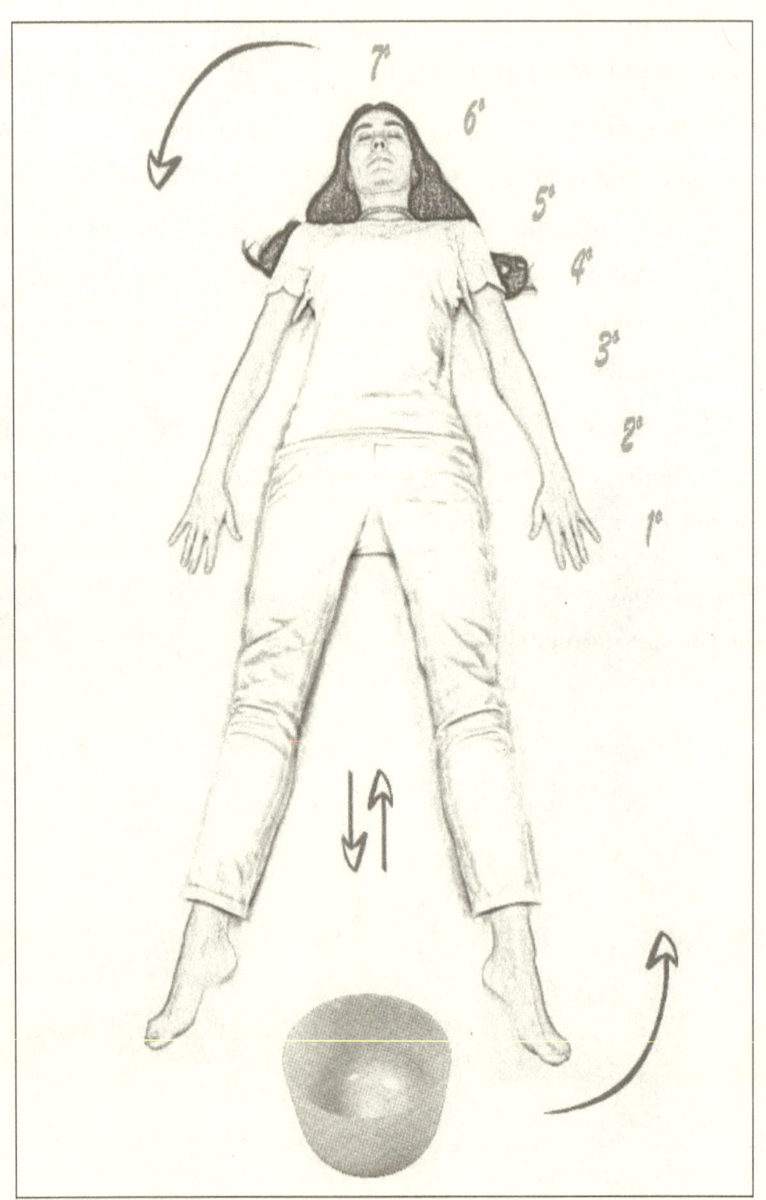

7°
6°
5°
4°
3°
2°
1°

Healing with multiple crystal bowls

The person lies on the floor on a mat or blanket and is covered with a white sheet or blanket.

We will ensure that the client is not wearing stones, watches, or metal objects, so as not to interfere with the therapy.

The therapist selects the bowls that will best aid the client's healing and place them around them, parallel to the chakras.

We will position the bowls 20 centimeters (8 inches) from the side of the client. The lowest-pitched bowls will be placed next to the first and second chakras, the medium-pitched bowls next to the third and fourth chakras, and the smallest, highest-pitched bowls next to the fifth, sixth, and seventh chakras.

- We will begin by activating the lowest-pitched bowl about 20 centimeters (8 inches) from the feet for about three minutes. It is important to let the bowl finish playing before moving on to harmonize the first chakra.
- We will move up the left side, starting with the first chakra, and continue sequentially through the remaining chakras until we reach the seventh.
- Then will move down the right side, harmonizing the sixth, fifth, fourth, third, second, and first chakras, finishing by harmonizing 20 centimeters from the feet.
- Once this activation around the body is complete, we will close the auric field, first activating the seventh chakra and then the point 20 centimeters from the feet.

We will finish by giving our client water to help them return to the present moment. Within sound therapy, it is possible to integrate other complementary therapies that enhance and enrich the healing process. One of the most widely used is gem therapy, which consists of the conscious use of minerals and crystals for their energetic and vibrational properties.

By placing a specific mineral on each chakra, the affinity between the crystal's vibration and the corresponding energy center is fostered.

When this work is combined with the sound of crystal bowls, a vibrational amplification effect occurs, as the sound acts as a vehicle that expands and distributes the mineral's energy throughout the energy field and the physical body.

Quartz crystal bowls, due to their crystalline composition, create a resonance particularly akin to that of minerals, facilitating a deeper and more harmonious integration of their healing qualities.

In this way, the sound vibration helps to unblock, balance, and activate the chakras, while the crystal supports and directs the energy work.

This combination allows for more complete and personalized sessions, tailored to each individual's needs, reinforcing both the energy work and the process of relaxation, presence, and inner listening.

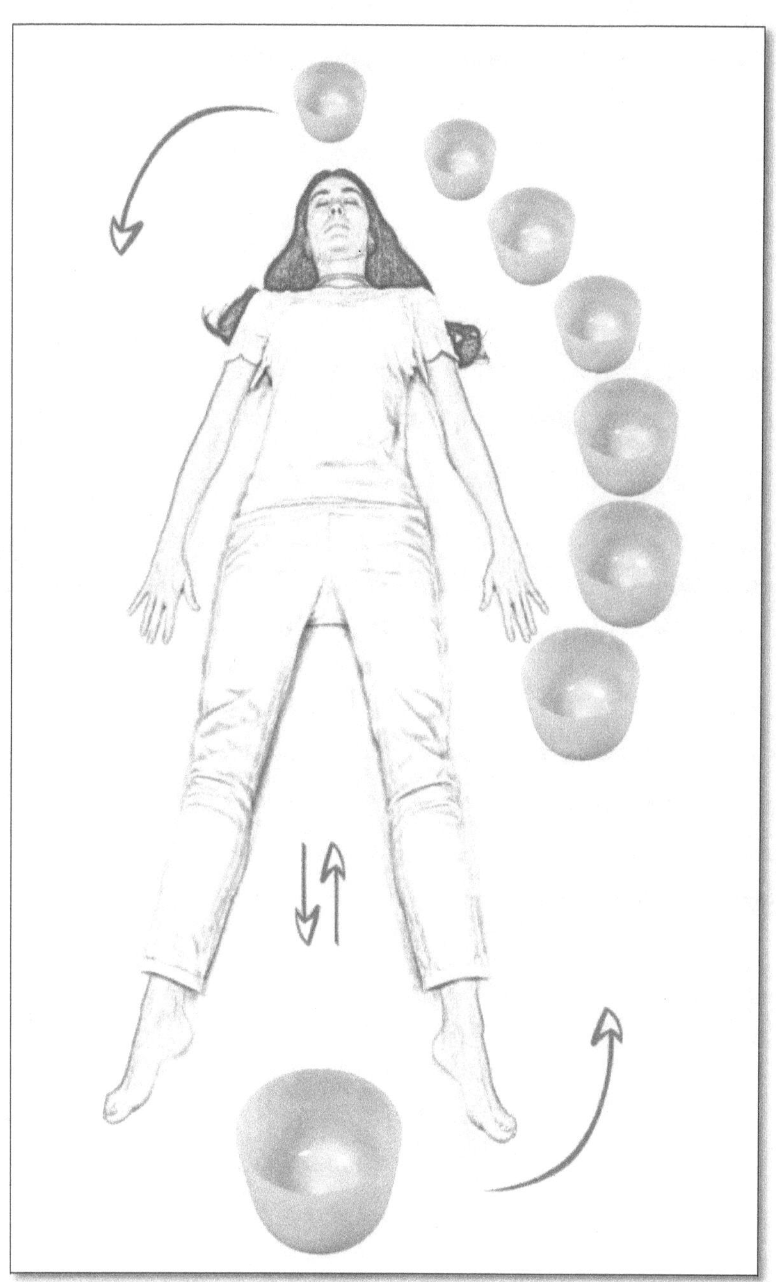

8.11 Case study

Pamela, forty-six years old and president of a fibromyalgia association, called us and told us she was very interested in trying the effectiveness of quartz crystal bowl sounds to alleviate the effects of the disease among her members.

We proposed a guided visualization accompanied by the harmonic sounds of quartz crystal bowls tuned to the "C" frequency to relax muscular and joint tension and achieve overall balance. At the same time, we would also activate the "A" frequency, which works on the nervous system, insomnia, and restlessness, to provide a state of deep relaxation. Pamela found the proposal appropriate, and we arranged to carry out the visualization the following week.

In the days that followed, we wrote a specific visualization to work on the different symptoms derived from this condition, lasting about 25 minutes, which, accompanied by the bowl frequencies, could have a total duration of about 50 minutes.

Fourteen people between forty and sixty years old attended the visualization, mostly women. We invited them to lie down comfortably on the floor and cover themselves with a blanket. We briefly explained the healing qualities of the bowls and that they would take part in a guided visualization to help alleviate the effects of their condition while the different bowl sounds were activated.

We warned them that they might feel restless and that, if uncomfortable, they could get up and leave the room. We also explained that they might fall asleep and that this would not prevent the healing effects of the bowl sounds from being integrated into their system, helping them in the same way. We began by activating the "C" with gentle strikes so they could connect with their bodies and relax through deep breathing. We then began the guided visualization, working on muscle relaxation.

Once relaxation of all the muscle chains was completed, we activated the "A" frequency to begin working on the central nervous system, releasing tension and fatigue and alleviating insomnia. In fact, at that point in the visualization, several participants fell deeply asleep.

We then alternated both sounds while continuing the visualization, in order to merge the benefits of both frequencies. Once the visualization was completed, slowly, and to the sound of the "C" frequency, we began returning to the present moment, bringing the session to an end.

The participants commented on their amazement at the sounds and vibrations transmitted by the bowls, and some expressed great gratitude, as they had been able to relax and even fall asleep, awakening with a sense of lightness and well-being.

A few days later, Pamela called me to arrange a monthly session, as the participants had told her the experience had been very gratifying. We agreed that working continuously would be very beneficial, as each session could focus on a specific symptom of the condition through guided visualization.

CHAPTER 9

TUNING FORKS

9.1 The history of tuning forks

Tuning forks were mainly used to tune musical instruments and also in physics classes to teach students about sound, vibration, and sound waves.In the medical field, tuning forks such as C 512 Hz were used to diagnose patients' hearing.

While higher-frequency tuning forks were used to examine hearing loss, others with lower frequencies, such as C 128 Hz, were used to test the sense of vibration as part of an examination of the peripheral nervous system. Likewise, some traumatologists and professionals use them to quickly diagnose whether a bone is broken, since when applied to the body, if there is a fracture, the pain is unbearable.

In the most advanced countries in the world, tuning forks have been replaced by complex electronic devices that perform the same function.

However, ideas and beliefs about tuning forks go much further back in history, reaching back to the ancient Greeks and Egyptians. Papyrus scrolls have been found with drawings of people holding something like a tuning fork.

In 1711, in England, the cavalry sergeant, trumpeter, and flutist John Shore devised the first tuning fork for musical purposes. It was made of steel and had a pitch of A (Do) 432.5 Hz.

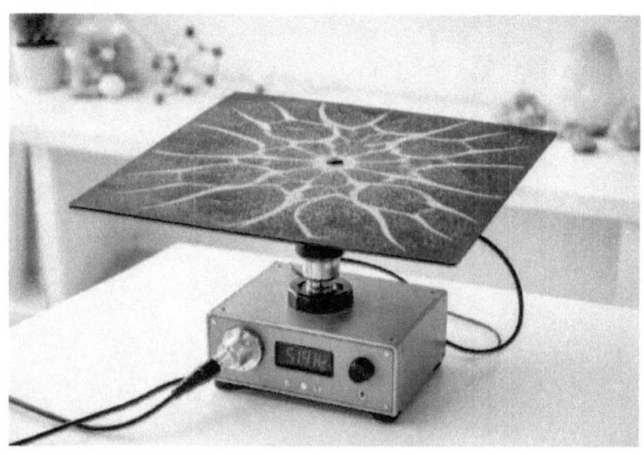

In 1800, the German physicist Ernst Chladni discovered that when a violin bow is drawn vertically along the edge of a metal plate sprinkled with sand, the sound waves produced create geometric patterns in the sand.

Depending on where the plate was activated, it created different frequencies that formed different geometric patterns in the sand. He built the first set of tuning forks based on the results of this experiment.

In 1834, J. H. Scheibler presented a series of 54 tuning forks covering a frequency spectrum between 220 and 440 Hz.

In 1863, the physiologist H. Helmholtz used a set of tuning forks with electromagnetic current for his experiments, in which people exposed to these sounds described the sensations produced by the different tones.

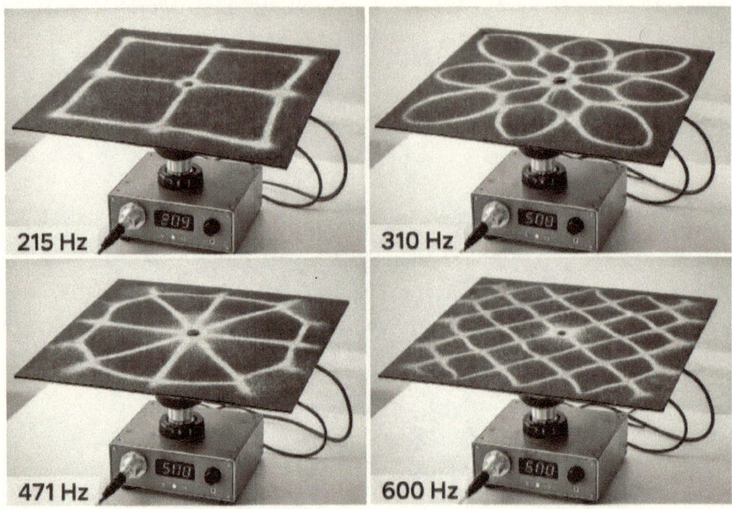

In the 1960s, the scientist Hans Jenny discovered that low-frequency sounds produced simple geometric shapes, and that as the sound frequency increased, the shapes became more complex.

He also discovered that the sound "Oh" produced a perfect circle, and that the sound "Om" produced a pattern similar to that of the ancient Hindu mandala known as the Sri Mandala.

In 1974, a professional jazz musician, Fabien Maman, realized that playing certain musical notes could produce different effects on the audience. He later studied traditional Chinese medicine and specialized in sound, music, and the human energy system, creating his own tuning forks.

Later, Fabien joined the prestigious researcher Helen Grimal at the National Center for Scientific Research in Paris to study the effects of sound on cancer cells and healthy cells, with incredible results.

In 1974, John Beaulieu, musician, osteopath, hypnologist, and polarity therapy specialist, discovered that tuning forks could be used to "tune" the nervous system.

In 1978, Arden Wilken and Jack Wilken, an English couple, created The School for Inner Sound, developing their own method of binaural healing with tuning forks tuned around the Schumann frequency.

In 1980, Barbara Hero, mathematician, musician, and artist, created the Lambdoma keyboard to help restore physical, emotional, mental, and spiritual well-being.

This program incorporates a very large number of frequencies, which Barbara determines based on mathematical studies and the complete work of Pythagoras. She derives the frequencies of organs, minerals, and meridians used to create the different tuning forks.

In 1982, Jonathan Goldman, musician and specialist in harmonic chanting, created the Sound Healers Association and incorporated tuning forks with Solfeggio frequencies into most of his healing compositions.

In 1987, Hans Cousto determined the vibrational frequencies of the planets in our Solar System based on mathematical calculations, confirming tones intuitively discovered by ancient cultures. These tones were later transferred to tuning forks.

In 1988, Dr. Robert Girard used the frequency 528 Hz to restore DNA.

In 1988, Dr. David Hulse rediscovered the ancient Solfeggio frequencies through his research based on the book *The Healing Codes* by biologist Dr. Leonard Horowitz and created SomaEnergetics.

In 2008, the International Tuning Fork Research Alliance was created by Drs. Larry Pannell, Charles Lightwalker, Helene Pelissier, Rick Boatright, John Beaulieu, Jan Longshore, Sandy Singh, Aminu Kazeem Olawale, Huang Yuanzhong, and Jan Morgans, to establish foundations and oversee research on tuning forks in the healing process.

9.2 Composition of a tuning fork

A tuning fork is an instrument, usually made of metal, shaped like a fork, which, when gently struck, vibrates and produces a specific, stable tone. For this reason, it is used in both music and sound therapy, as it allows for working with precise frequencies.

Therapeutic tuning forks can be made from different materials; the most common are steel (stainless or chrome-plated) and aluminum. Both materials transmit vibration effectively, although they differ in their sound characteristics.

Aluminum tuning forks produce a higher volume of sound, while steel tuning forks, being denser, maintain their vibration for longer.

Aluminum tuning forks can be found with or without weights at their ends. Weighted tuning forks are especially recommended for applying directly to denser points or areas of the body, such as bones and muscles, as their vibration is transmitted more deeply and sustainably.

Weightless tuning forks emit a higher volume of sound and are often used in therapies focused on working with energetic or subtle bodies, primarily acting on the vibrational field surrounding the body

There are also tuning forks made of quartz crystal or alloys with a high content of precious metals, such as gold. However, these types of tuning forks are not commonly used in sound healing, as they do not offer a wide range of vibrational frequencies.

In recent years, gemstones and minerals have been incorporated into some tuning forks to enhance and refine their frequency. In some models, the gemstone is embedded in the upper part of the prong, while

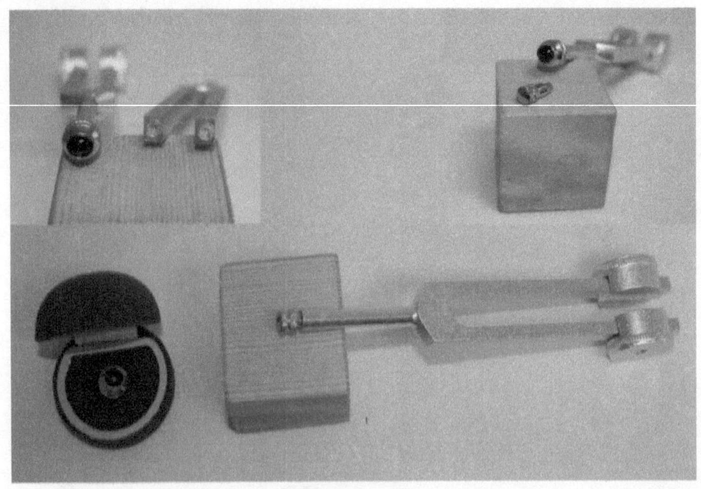

in others it is screwed onto the tip, allowing the sound vibration to be combined with the energetic properties of the mineral.

9.3 Tuning fork models

The shape varies very little. Differences are mainly found in the length, the shape of the handle, and whether the prongs are round, square, or rectangular. There is also a clear distinction between weighted and unweighted tuning forks.

When a tuning fork is activated by striking it against a hard surface or object, it vibrates at a fundamental note. First, the fundamental note is heard, a nearly pure sound, and then its corresponding harmonics.

Since the vibrational properties of a tuning fork depend exclusively on its shape and the material used, the sinusoidal wave it generates always maintains its tuning.

9.4 Parts of a tuning fork

Take the tuning fork in your hand and let us name each part.

- There are two prongs that create the vibration of the tuning fork.

- The upper part of the prongs is called the top.

- The point where the two prongs join is called the yoke.

- The part that extends downward from the yoke is the handle, which is where the tuning fork is held for activation.

- At the end of the handle is the tip.

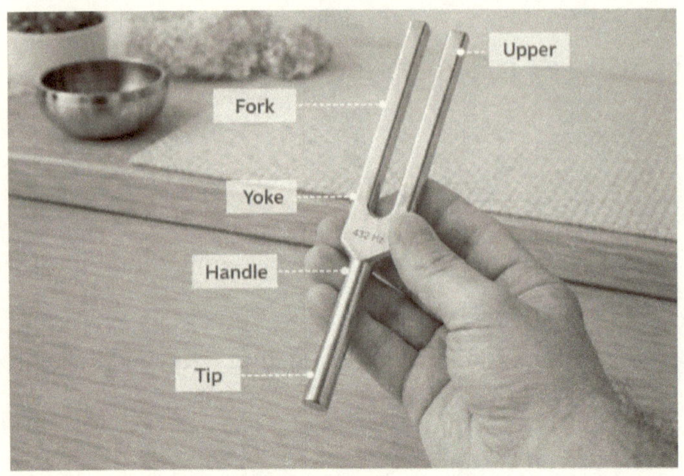

9.5 Types of Tuning Forks

There is a wide range of tuning forks for therapeutic purposes, all based on different theories used to calculate their frequencies.

Below are those most used in therapy, although as therapists continue to work with them, their use expands and new frequencies are created:

1. 528 Hz

2. Chi (Qi) Activation

3. Adam Qadmon

4. DNA Nucleotide

5. Archangels

6. Angelic

7. Energetic Support

8. Bio-Resonance

9. Kabbalah – Tree of Life

10. Brain

11. Chakras

12. Blood Circulation

13. Basic Chromo therapy

14. Chromo therapy of the Spirit

15. Quartz

16. Dan Tien

17. Harmonic Spectrum / Musical Notes

18. Fibonacci

19. Genesis / Creation

20. Meridians

21. Minerals

22. Sustained Notes

23. Om

24. Human Organs

25. Otto

26. Ozone

27. Phi Ratio

28. Planets

29. Cellulite Reduction

30. Nervous System

31. Solfeggio

32. I Am That I Am

33. YHWH – The Tuning Fork of God

34. Yin & Yang

9.6 Holding a Tuning Fork

Hold the tuning fork by the handle between the thumb and index finger, gently but firmly.

If you feel you need more grip, include the middle finger.

The wrist should remain relaxed.

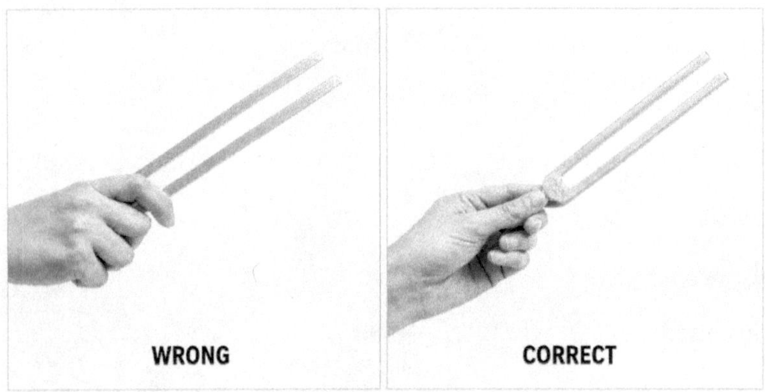

One of the benefits of using unweighted tuning forks is that, because they are lighter, they cause less fatigue when holding them. The lighter the tuning fork, the more comfortable it will be for your fingers, hands, and wrist. This is something to consider if you suffer from arthritis in any of these areas.

A session that feels uncomfortable will restrict the energetic flow between you and your client.

9.7 Activating the Tuning Fork

For the tuning fork to activate and vibrate, it must be struck with a firm, decisive blow against a hard surface.

We recommend beginning practice with an unweighted tuning fork, striking it against different surfaces to notice the differences in vibration and to gain skill and confidence in handling it.

Some of the surfaces against which a tuning fork can be struck include:

- The side of the palm of the hand.

- The thigh, about a hand's width above the knee. There is incorrect and dangerous information circulating on the internet suggesting that the tuning fork be struck on the kneecap. Do NOT do this under any circumstances, as you can cause serious injury with significant consequences.

- On a protective pad placed over the top of the knee.

- With a rubber mallet.

- With the flat side of a rubber mallet.

- With a wooden mallet.

- With a rubber activator.

- On the edge of a massage table padded with foam and leather or faux leather.

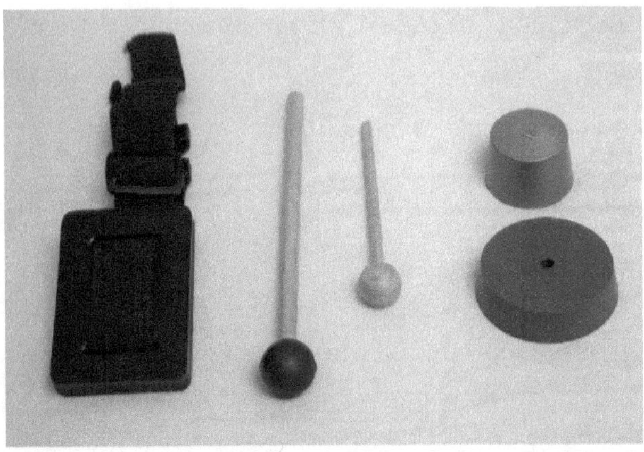

The harder the surface you choose, the higher, sharper, and shorter the vibration will be. The softer the surface you choose to activate your tuning fork, the more comforting, muted, deeper, and longer lasting the vibration will be.

9.8 Proper use and care of the tuning fork

What most affects the pitch of a tuning fork is temperature. The pitch of a tuning fork can drop by 1 percent for every 7°C increase or decrease in temperature

Be careful not to take them out of your home's room temperature and forget them in the car, whether in winter or summer, or leave them near a radiator.

Strong impacts also affect them, such as when they fall onto hard ceramic floors, when they are struck extremely hard against each other, or when they are stored together without individual cases. This can cause small dents or deep scratches that affect their precise frequency.

Cleaning and storage

Store your tuning forks in a dry, clean place. Remember that pitch varies with temperature, so keep them where the ambient temperature remains stable.

Excessive humidity can cause discoloration in aluminum tuning forks and oxidation in steel ones. Do not use chemical products such as detergents, ammonia, or similar substances to clean your tuning fork. Simply wipe it with damp cloth and then dry it thoroughly.

You can store your tuning forks in their original pouches, wrapped in cotton inside a wooden box, or place them upright in a wooden block with holes designed for this purpose.

9.9 The correct activation of the tuning fork

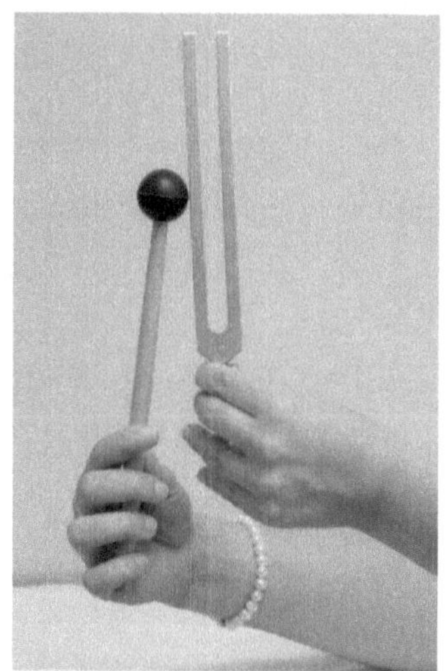

In addition to the surface used to activate it, the point where the tuning fork receives the strike also affects the quality, sharpness, and volume of the vibration.In unweighted tuning forks, the closer you strike to the top, the sharper and stronger the vibration will be the closer you strike to the yoke, the more muted and weaker the vibration will be.

In general terms, the ideal place to strike the tuning fork is approximately halfway between the yoke and the top.

In weighted tuning forks, the strike should be applied directly to the center of the weight, preferably using a rubber activator.

9.10 Duration of the tuning fork at each point

Once the tuning fork is activated and placed on the point you wish to work on, the ideal time to remain there is about 20–30 seconds, or until you feel that the tuning fork has stopped vibrating between your fingers.

It is possible that the strike used to activate it was too soft and the tuning fork stopped vibrating before 20 seconds, or that contact with something interrupted the vibration. In that case, you should reactivate it before the 20 seconds have elapsed.

You will stop feeling the vibration in your hand before the tuning fork actually stops vibrating. For this reason, it is recommended that you count to ten before reactivating it, because even if you no longer feel it, the subtle vibration is still present.

We must have enough practice so that the vibration of our tuning forks is uniform and so that we place them on the body with the same pressure and at the same distance from the ears.

If you have performed a chakra balance on three different people within a short period of time—two or three days—and in all three cases the same chakras appear affected, it means that you yourself are also experiencing that imbalance in some way. You will need to work on it personally to understand what is happening in that area of your life. Subtly, you are projecting your own issues.

The body is very wise and always seeks balance. It only absorbs the amount of vibration it needs to unblock or harmonize itself, and once it has received enough, it emits signs of restlessness—such as changes in breathing or other bodily signals—to indicate that it is sufficient.

When a client expresses that a vibration has produced a certain emotional state, they are communicating and bringing out an emotion that was unconscious. This is positive, because once it is conscious, it is easier to work with.

You may position yourself on the client's left or right side, but always in a way that is comfortable for you. You can choose to begin working from the feet to the head or vice versa. Your intuition will guide you in deciding what is best for you and your client.

Do not be rigid when working with energy. Allow yourself to be flexible and open to learning new techniques and ways of working with energy. Both you and your client will benefit from this.

Energy therapists without an artistic or creative sense are merely technicians who know the effects of their techniques and tools. It is essential to work from the heart and to be very attentive to how you hold the tuning forks, how you place them, and to your relationship with the client and the environment during the session.

Since these healing sessions are for the client's enjoyment and well-being, not ours, we must remember that sometimes a client may become agitated by certain sounds. In such cases, those specific sounds should be made deeper, softer, and slower, or even avoided until a future session.

For people who are very ill or in strong disharmony, it is advisable to use low, muted tones for healing. Gradually, over successive sessions and as they recover, the pitch of the tuning forks can be increased.

Likewise, you may notice that a client needs a more "powerful" frequency. In that case, you will activate your tuning fork on a harder surface.

9.11 Uses of tuning forks

Tuning forks, like other sound instruments, can be used not only in therapy but also for many other purposes, such as:

- Transmuting stagnant or negative energies in a place, home, office, car, etc.

- Cleaning crystals, gemstones, stones, or any other object of your choice.

- Working with pets, on their energetic points, meridians, chakras, etc.

- Working in the aura of plants.

- Energizing food and water.

- Enhancing ceremonies and rituals.

9.12 Tuning forks for beginners

As mentioned previously, there is a wide variety of tuning forks, and new frequencies are added every year. To begin working with them in a simple and effective way, we have selected those we consider fundamental.

Om Tuning Fork

The Om tuning fork is also known as the COSMIC Om and is related to the frequency of the heart. In some chakra systems, the heart chakra has the same frequency as Om.

This frequency is not based on the musical scale, but was decoded by Hans Cousto, who calculated it based on the year, or the 365 days the Earth takes to orbit the Sun.

It is wonderful for meditation, traveling to other dimensions, energy sessions, or simply tuning into universal energy. It relaxes, harmonizes, grounds, soothes, and calms. Hindu mystics were given this tone when they entered meditation and opened themselves to the cosmos.

The music of the sitar and tambura is tuned to this note, called *sadja*, which means "the father of the others," the eternal tone that never stops and vibrates at 136.1 Hz.

Physically tuning your body to the Om vibration is entering a state of integral balance specific to healing and higher states of consciousness.

It helps to:

- Center body and mind.

- Help meditators and yoga practitioners reach their desired state more easily.

- Improve breathing.

- Relieve bodily tension.

- Control pain.

- Facilitate yoga postures.

- Mobilize disharmony and tension in the body to restore well-being.

528 Hz tuning fork

Currently, the notes we use to compose music come from a scale known as the diatonic scale, but before the 16th century, the Solfeggio scale was used. It consisted of six notes with the following frequencies:

TUNING FORK	FREQUENCY	CONCEPT
Ut	396 Hz	Release of guilt and fear
Re	417 Hz	Transmutation, facilitates change and creativity
Mi	528 Hz	Miracles and DNA repair
Fa	639 Hz	Enhances communication, understanding, tolerance, and love. Interpersonal relationships
Sol	741 Hz	Solves problems, develops intuition, and facilitates self-expression
La	852 Hz	Communication with spiritual beings and return to spiritual order. Pineal gland activation

These original notes were used in ancient Gregorian chants. It was believed that special chants imparted tremendous spiritual blessings when sung in harmony during religious services.

These powerful frequencies were rediscovered by Dr. Joseph Puleo, as explained by Dr. Leonard Horowitz—a Harvard-educated, award-winning scientist—in his book *Healing Codes for the Biological Apocalypse*.

The third note, the 528 Hz frequency, corresponds to the note Mi in this scale and comes from the Latin expression *miraculous* which means "miracle."

Interestingly, this is the same frequency that biochemical geneticists use to repair DNA, the genetic pattern upon which life is based.

This frequency has the following characteristics:

- It is the difference between love and war.

- It is the locomotive energy of universal abundance, the bioenergy of health and longevity.

- It is the harmonic vibration of self-esteem.

- It opens and elevates your heart.

- It is the essence of perfect love. When you are in this frequency, you are tuned to your creative spirit, and everything flows in perfect rhythm.

According to Dr. Leonard Horowitz, there is a special sound in unconditional love, the frequency 528 Hz:

'We know that the frequency of love, 528 Hz, is among the six most creative frequencies in the universe, because mathematics does not lie. The geometry of physical

reality universally reflects this music. These findings have been independently derived, peer-reviewed, and empirically validated."

Being in contact with this frequency can help open the heart, promote peace, and accelerate healing. The 528 Hz tuning fork is applied using the techniques we already know: on the ears, chakras, meridians, reflex points, etc.

Beautiful musical compositions have been created with the 528 Hz frequency as a background, which you can listen to while reading or meditating, allowing you to feel its benefits. We have prepared a selection of these compositions for you, available through the following link or QR code.

You can also access it from this link:

https://thewingbook.com/bonus/sound_therapy/

Angelic tuning forks

The creation of these exquisite tuning forks is credited to John Beaulieu. They open the soul to the angelic realm and allow us to become a channel to transmit and receive cosmic energies through the Sun.

The Toltec tradition says that the Sun of our Solar System is a two-way conduit between the cosmos and our planet.

Angelic tuning forks are based on the ninth octave of the harmonic series. In the harmonic series, a fundamental tone creates a second tone, the second creates a third, and so on. They rise in pitch and resemble the *Stairway to Heaven*.

They can be used individually or together to enhance meditation, and they can be used to amplify the energies of crystals.

They can be activated individually with a wooden mallet or by striking them very lightly against each other. In this case, the higher-frequency tuning forks are held between the fingers and lightly struck with the crystal tuning fork or the 4,096 Hz tuning fork.

When they are activated simultaneously, an angelic concert is created.

The Angelic Kit consists of three tuning forks with the following frequencies:

- 4,096 Hz – crystal tuning fork

- 4,160 Hz

- 4,225 Hz

The three tuning forks activated simultaneously are used, among other things for:

- Cleansing a person's aura of dense energy.
- Cleansing rooms.
- Cleansing the bed after a night of nightmares.
- Purifying food of preservatives and chemicals.

- Cleansing newly purchased items.
- Cleansing gifts.
- Purifying ley lines, Hartmann crossings, and energy vortices.
- Cleansing the aura of plants, trees, hedges, etc.
- Cleansing the aura of pets.

Chakra system tuning forks

Each chakra has a "standard" vibrational frequency, and each of our chakras vibrates at a specific frequency within that standard range.

When one of our chakras moves outside these parameters, it indicates discomfort at the physical, emotional, mental, and/or spiritual level.

We can restore well-being to the affected chakra so that it returns to its optimal frequency by exposing it to its appropriate vibration through the principle of forced resonance.

There is ongoing controversy when it comes to determining the "standard" frequency of each chakra. To date, sound therapists have leaned toward three systems, the most widely used in practice being the one tuned to planetary frequencies.

CHAKRA	PLANETARY CHAKRA SET	HARMONIC SPECTRUM SET	SOLFEGGIO SET
Root	Day/ Earth (194,18 Hz)	C (256 Hz)	Ut (396 Hz)
Sacral	Moon (210,42 Hz)	D (288 Hz)	D (417 Hz)

Solar Plexus	Sun (126,22 Hz)	E (320 Hz)	E (528 Hz)
Heart	Earth/Sun - Om (136,10 Hz)	F (341,3 Hz)	F (639 Hz)
Throat	Mercury (141,27 Hz)	G (384 Hz)	G (741 Hz)
Third Eye	Venus (221,23 Hz)	A (426,7 Hz)	A (852 Hz)
Crown	Platonic Year (172,06 Hz)	B (480 Hz)	—

These tuning fork kits are associated with the chakra system, and the difference between them is that they work on the energy centers from different planes of being. This differentiation allows the vibrational work to be adapted to the specific needs of each person and each therapeutic process.

The Chakra Kit, based on planetary movements and correspondences, uses deeper, lower frequencies. These vibrations have a direct effect on the physical plane, helping to work on the body, structure, organs, and tissues. It is a kit especially indicated for processes where grounding, body regulation, and support for physical symptoms are needed.

The Harmonic Spectrum Kit acts in a more subtle way. Although it also harmonizes the chakras, its focus is more oriented towards the mental and energetic planes. This kit promotes internal organization, mental clarity, balance of the energy field, and coherence between thought, emotion, and vibration.

The Solfeggio Kit works with a series of frequencies traditionally associated with processes of profound transformation. Although it also affects the chakra system, its action is primarily focused on the emotional and spiritual planes. These frequencies facilitate emotional release, the healing of deep-seated memories, and connection to higher states of consciousness.

In short, all the sets harmonize the chakra system, but each does so at a different level. This diversity of approaches allows the therapist to choose the most appropriate tool depending on the moment, the session's objective, and the client's overall state, offering a more precise, conscious, and comprehensive sound healing experience.

9.13 Tuning fork application techniques

There are various healing techniques using tuning forks, but they are generally grouped into two categories: those involving direct contact with the body and those involving indirect application without touching it. Here we will see an example of each so you can begin practicing safely and confidently.

Direct body contact technique

- Holding the tuning fork by the handle, activate it and place the tip of the handle on the body for 20 or 30 seconds.
- Some people first place the tuning fork on the body and then activate it: this is incorrect practice, as it does not vibrate the same way and the client will feel the impact.
- Here you must be mindful of the pressure you apply to the body. If you are unsure whether the pressure is optimal for the client, you should ask them, and depending on their response, you will loosen or increase the pressure.

- The client should feel the vibration, but not in a heavy or "stabbing" way.

- The direct contact technique is often applied for various purposes, as we will discuss in the following personal practice examples.

The ear technique

Sound reaches the brain more quickly through the ears, which is very useful due to its speed and simplicity.

You can use a single tuning fork and pass it from one ear to the other, circling the head, not the face. Alternatively, you can use a tuning fork simultaneously for each ear and then switch hands so that both vibrations reach both ears equally. Turn on the tuning forks and gently and slowly place them about 20 centimeters from the client's ear. Slowly move them closer to about 10 centimeters, at which point you ask if they can hear it and are comfortable.

If they say they can't hear it, then slowly move closer to no more than 5 centimeters and ask again, until you identify the distance at which the client is comfortable.

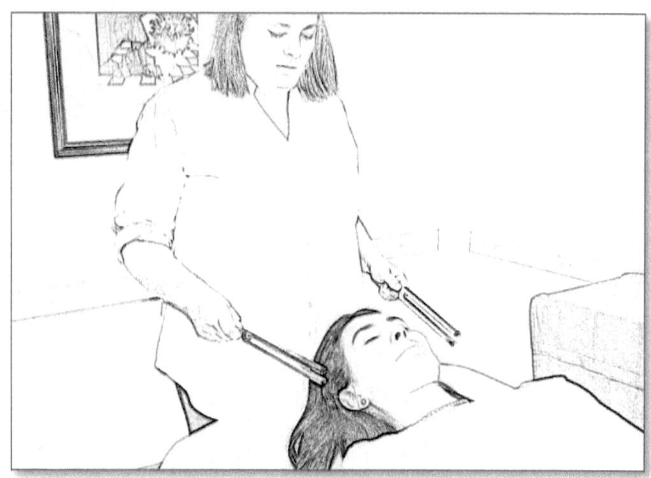

It is essential that people with long hair tie it back with a hair tie so that it does not interfere with the therapy by muffling the sound or vibration of the tuning fork.

9.14 Exercise with tuning forks

To better understand what your client might feel, practice the different placements on yourself. Place the vibrating tip of the tuning fork on:

- A reflexology point, acupuncture point, chakra, etc.
- A muscle.
- A bone.
- The outer side of a glass filled with water.
- The back of a quartz crystal point, to focus the energy from the point to a specific area.
- A crystal placed over a chakra, to introduce the crystal's vibration more quickly.
- Applying the "Healing Specific Points" Technique

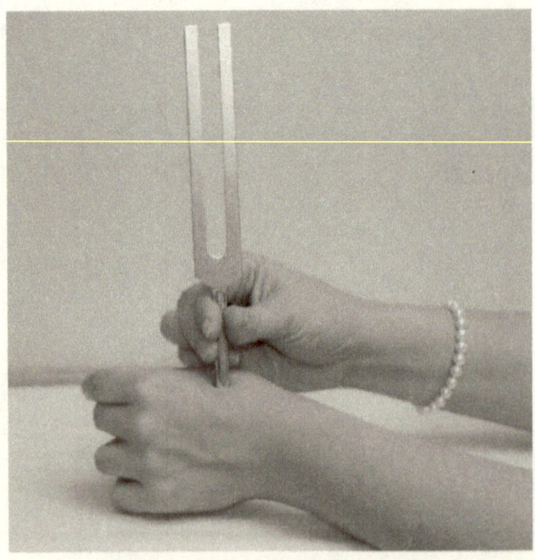

9.15 The Om tuning fork as a "Rescue Remedy"

Always keep an Om tuning fork handy to relieve stress and energize yourself.

- Activate the tuning fork and place it on each ear for 20 seconds, breathing deeply and relaxedly. Repeat three times.
- Activate the tuning fork and place it on the third eye chakra for 20 seconds. Repeat three times.
- Activate the tuning fork and place it behind the head at the level of the first cervical vertebra for 20 seconds. Repeat three times.
- Activate the tuning fork and place it on the heart chakra for 20 seconds. Repeat three times.

9.16 Healing techniques with tuning forks

Chakra harmonization with the direct contact technique

For this harmonization, the client should be face down or seated if necessary.

• We begin harmonizing the chakras from the root chakra. Hold the tuning fork corresponding to this chakra, activate it, and place the tip of the handle on the body, at the level of the root chakra, for a minimum of 20 seconds.

• Repeat this harmonization two more times to complete a series of three. In this way, each chakra is harmonized with its corresponding vibration for approximately one minute.

• Here, we must be mindful of the pressure we apply to the body. If we are unsure whether the pressure is optimal for the client, we should ask them and, depending on their response, loosen or increase the pressure.

• We perform the same procedure we used for the root chakra for the other chakras.

Chakra Harmonization with the Ear Technique

• Hold the C tuning fork, for the root chakra, in your left hand and the D tuning fork, for the sacral chakra, in your right hand.

• Activate them consecutively or simultaneously and then place them about 20 centimeters from the ears. Slowly move them closer until they are about 10 centimeters away, at which point you ask the client if they can hear it and are comfortable.

• If they say they can't hear it, then slowly move closer, no more than 5 centimeters away, and ask again, until you identify the distance at which the client is comfortable.

• Once you've identified the distance and 20 seconds have passed, reactivate the sensors and begin moving closer to their ears from a distance of 20 centimeters, until you reach the distance at which the client can hear.

• Repeat this tuning process two more times to complete a series of three. Then, switch the tuning forks to the other hand and repeat the same procedure.

• Once the series of three is complete, keep the C tuning fork in your hand and switch from D to E for the solar plexus chakra, and begin the series of three with the C and E tuning forks.

• After completing the series, switch the tuning forks back and repeat the same procedure.

Continue this practice until you complete the series with C for the root chakra and B for the crown chakra.

9.17 Case Study

Paul, thirty-four years old, came to consultation while going through a traumatic divorce. He felt deep sadness and a lack of self-esteem that prevented him from living his daily life normally. Increasingly often, he questioned the purpose of his life, and this sense of despair led him to have self-destructive thoughts that frightened him more and more.

We explained that when one chakra is out of balance, another automatically compensates. Clearly, his heart chakra was affected, as he did not feel worthy of love; his solar plexus chakra, because his self-esteem was compromised; and his root chakra, due to suicidal thoughts. The remaining chakras were compensating.

Therefore, the most appropriate therapy was a general chakra harmonization, placing special emphasis on the three chakras mentioned above. Paul was willing to try our suggestion, as his suffering was immense. He removed all metal objects and lay comfortably on the treatment table.

We decided to work with the traditional chakra kit, which is tuned to the planets that energize the chakras, and to apply the horizontal and spiral techniques. We began by performing a chakra harmonization using the horizontal technique, starting with the root chakra and finishing with the crown chakra.

Once completed, we took the tuning fork for the root chakra and used the spiral technique, starting at a distance of 50 centimeters and moving clockwise to increase its energy. We approached the chakra, gradually reducing the diameter until reaching a couple of centimeters from it. We repeated this process three times before moving on to the solar plexus chakra tuning fork and performing the same procedure there.

When we finished with the solar plexus chakra, we moved up to the heart chakra, using the corresponding tuning fork and repeating the same process as with the previous two chakras. Throughout the entire session, Paul was restless, which we interpreted as a sign of energetic unblocking. We felt the need to connect the energies of the different chakras, so we decided to close the auric field and the session using the rolling technique.

For this, we used two OM tuning forks. Starting from the feet and moving toward the head, we enveloped the energy of the root chakra with that of the sacral, then the solar plexus, the heart, the throat, the third eye, and the crown, repeating the sequence two more times.

Once finished, we considered it necessary to let him rest for about five minutes so that all the mobilized energy could settle. After this time, César spontaneously opened his eyes, and his expression reflected deep relaxation.

He began to cry and said that although he still felt deep sadness, he also felt liberated, with a renewed desire to live. Paul decided to attend sessions once a week. After seven sessions, he felt emotionally balanced enough and motivated to reclaim his life.

CHAPTER 10

A SOUND HEALING SESSION

There is a way to prepare any therapeutic session that varies slightly depending on the type of therapy being practiced. At its core, it's based on observation and common sense... although we all know that common sense can be quite subjective too.

In the QR code, you'll find complementary material where we explain in greater depth the key aspects you should keep in mind to ensure your session is a success—both for you and for your client.

Every therapy has its own distinctive elements that are important to consider at the beginning and at the end of a session. Now, we're going to focus specifically on how to approach these in Sound healing.

10.1 Things to keep in mind

No two sessions are ever the same because neither two people are the same, or in other words, no two energy systems are identical. You may follow the same protocol, but the outcome will always be different.

It's essential to have enough practice so that the vibration of the instruments is steady and harmonious. If you place them on the body, apply a consistent level of pressure each time. If you want the vibration to work through the auditory system, position them at an equal distance from the ears, making sure the sound is never uncomfortable.

The body is wise and naturally moves toward balance. For this reason, the client will only integrate the amount of vibration needed to release blockages or restore harmony.

The client will also let you know when they've received the necessary vibrations through subtle signs such as restlessness, changes in breathing, or small shifts in body posture.

When a client says that a certain vibration activates a specific emotional state, what's really happening is that an emotion that was previously unconscious is becoming conscious. And that's a good thing, because once a blockage comes into awareness, it becomes much more accessible for integration and healing.

You may position yourself on the client's left or right side, whichever feels most comfortable for you.

Avoid working with rigidity. Stay flexible so the vibrations can flow through you naturally and reach the client's energy system or chakras with ease.

Most commonly, sessions begin from the feet and move toward the head, ensuring grounding first before working with the upper centers.

However, in some cases it may be more appropriate to begin from the head and move down toward the feet, especially if you sense the person arrives overly "ungrounded" or scattered and needs to settle first.

Your intuition and experience will guide you toward what is most appropriate in each situation.

10.2 Opening the session

We open and close our Sound healing sessions using the same technique. What changes is the treatment we carry out in between, as it will always depend on the client's specific needs.

Once the client is comfortably settled—lying on the treatment table, on the floor, or seated on a chair, as previously agreed—we begin by gently and harmoniously opening their energy field.

There are many ways to do this opening, and with practice you'll discover the one that feels most natural to you. Below, we explain how we do it:

1. Hold the OM tuning fork.

2. Activate it.

3. Slowly move it about 30 centimeters (12 inches) away from the body, starting at the feet.

4. Move upward along the left side of the body.

5. Gently circle around the head.

6. Move down along the right side until you return to the feet.

7. From there, move upward through the center of the body, passing through all the chakras, and then descend again along the same central line until you finish once more at the feet—the point where you began.

8. During the process, reactivate the tuning fork whenever necessary, always avoiding doing so near the ears or the head.

10.3 Sound treatment

After the opening, the sound healing begins. At this point, questions may arise, since there are many instruments that can be used in a session, and it's not always obvious which one is the most appropriate in each case.

Our recommendation is to let yourself be guided by your intuition. On an unconscious level, we often sense what is most suitable for each client.

That said, we'd like to share our experience and offer you some practical guidance on how to use the instruments mentioned in this book:

- **Tibetan bowls and percussion instruments:** More suitable for working with physical ailments, both because of their composition and the way they are applied.

- **Tuning forks and voice:** Especially effective for addressing imbalances in the energetic and emotional body.

- **Quartz bowls:** Due to their vibrational qualities, they are particularly appropriate for working with emotional and spiritual disharmonies.

We apply this same approach in our sound concerts, where we combine Tibetan bowls, voice, and quartz bowls with the intention of harmonizing the physical, emotional, mental, and spiritual levels.

10.4 Closing the session

Once the sound treatment has been completed, you are ready to close the session. As mentioned earlier, you can do this by following the same eight steps described in the opening.

This closing of the energy field is usually done with the OM tuning fork, although you may also use a low-pitched Tibetan bowl or even your voice.

If you wish, you can perform the closing with the client standing. In that case, it's advisable to begin at the feet, move upward along the back, gently circle around the head, and then descend along the front of the body to finish once again at the feet.

The closing process can be repeated as many times as you feel the client needs.

This technique helps seal the auric field and harmonize the chakras, supporting them in returning to their appropriate size and balance before the person leaves your practice.

At the end of the treatment, make sure the client is well grounded and fully present. Approach gently and let them know you are going to lightly touch their shoulders to avoid startling them, informing them that the session has come to an end.

Invite them to take their time getting up and leave a glass of water nearby for them to drink, helping them reconnect with the "here and now."

It's essential that the client leaves feeling grounded and has enough time to integrate the vibrational frequencies they've been exposed to, as these continue working on different levels even after the session has finished.

10.5 Sound as an integrative tool

One of the great strengths of Sound healing is its capacity for integration. Sound can be used as a primary therapy, but also as a complement to other therapeutic approaches.

Its application is broad and adaptable. For example, you can close a reflexology session by using tuning forks to harmonize the energy field after physical work. In the same way, you can begin a psychology session by helping the client relax with Tibetan bowls, encouraging greater emotional openness and receptivity.

Sound does not compete with other therapies; it enhances them. It prepares the ground, deepens the process, and supports integration of what has been worked through.

In all cases, it's essential to inform the client about the instruments you will be using and to obtain their prior consent. Clarity and respect strengthen trust and are a fundamental part of the therapeutic framework.

Sound is always available. As a tool, as a bridge, and as a guide. The rest you will discover through practice, listening, and experience.

Trust the process.

A WARM FAREWELL

Dear Reader,

We have reached the end of this shared journey, a path of listening, presence, and discovery through sound and vibration.

We hope that within these pages you have found understanding, clarity, and practical resources to approach the power of frequencies as tools for balance and harmonization.

Throughout this book, we have explored how sound acts beyond what is audible, how vibrations dialogue with the body, emotions, and mind, and how they can accompany us through deep processes of regulation and well-being.

Sound does not impose or force; it simply invites the organism to remember its own capacity for order and coherence. Each session, each conscious application of sound, is an opportunity to pause, listen, and allow the body to respond from its own wisdom. Intention and the quality of listening are just as important as the instrument being used, it is there that the real work takes place.

We hope that what you have learned here accompanies you both in your practice and in your everyday life, and that you can integrate sound as a close and effective ally. May every vibration you apply be an act of deep respect for the body and its rhythms.

Sound is a bridge between the visible and the invisible, a frequency that organizes, supports, and harmonizes. And every person who works with it, whether for themselves or for others, becomes a conscious channel of balance.

If you feel that this book has resonated with you and you wish to go deeper, scan the QR code you will find here. Through it, you will gain access to training and resources that expand and support sound work, helping you integrate this practice in a more conscious and structured way.

Everything we have offered in this book and in the QR code attachments we have created to accompany you on this journey are made with the same intention: to accompany you, support you and remind you that balance is a state to which you can always return.

With all our affection and gratitude,

Mercedes Cadarso Sanchez...... Maria Socastro Gonzalez

REFERENCES

Beaulieu, J. (2010). *Human Tuning: Sound Healing with Tuning Forks.* BioSonic Enterprises.

Beaulieu, J. (2010). *Music and Sound in the Healing Arts.* BioSonic Enterprises.

Campbell, D. G. (Ed.). (1991). *Music: Physician for Times to Come.* Quest Books.

Cousto, H. (2015). *The Cosmic Octave: Origin of Harmony.* Life Rhythm.

D'Angelo, J. (1994). *Healing with the Voice.* Destiny Books.

Gaynor, M. L. (1999). *Sounds of Healing: A Physician Reveals the Therapeutic Power of Sound, Voice, and Music.* Broadway Books.

Gibson, D. (2019). *The Complete Guide to Sound Healing.* Sound Healing Center Press.

Goldman, J. (2002). *Healing Sounds: The Power of Harmonics.* Inner Traditions.

Goldman, J. (2010). *The 7 Secrets of Sound Healing.* New World Library.

Harner, M. (1990). *The Way of the Shaman.* HarperOne.

Hess, T. (2013). *Singing Bowls: A Practical Handbook of Tibetan Bowl Sound Healing.* Lotus Press.

Huyser, A. (2012). *Tibetan Singing Bowls: A Practical Guide*. Destiny Books.

Jenny, H. (2001). *Cymatics: A Study of Wave Phenomena and Vibration*. MACROmedia Publishing.

Leeds, J. (2001). *The Power of Sound: How to Be Healthy and Productive Using Music and Sound*. Healing Arts Press.

Maman, F. (1997). *The Tao of Sound: Healing with Sound Frequencies*. Tama-Do Press.

Maman, F. (2014). *Sound Healing with Acupuncture*. Tama-Do Press.

Michaels, A. (2014). *The Singing Bowl Book*. Temple Lodge Publishing.

Miller, R. (2010). *The Healing Drum: African Wisdom Teachings*. Destiny Books.

Muller, A., & Lauterborn, W. (2009). *Acoustic Resonance and Sound Healing*. Springer.

Neher, A. (1962). *A Physiological Explanation of Unusual Behavior in Ceremonies Involving Drums*. Human Biology Journal.

Peters, G. (2016). *Quartz Crystal Singing Bowls: Sound Healing for Body, Mind and Spirit*. Crystal Sound Publications.

Rossing, T. D. (2000). *Science of Percussion Instruments*. World Scientific.

Shamai, M. (2011). *Drumming as a Therapeutic Tool*. Jessica Kingsley Publishers.

Tomatis, A. (1991). *The Conscious Ear*. Station Hill Press.

Wigram, T., Pedersen, I. N., & Bonde, L. O. (2002). *A Comprehensive Guide to Music HEALING*. Jessica Kingsley Publishers.

www.ingramcontent.com/pod-product-compliance
Lightning Source LLC
Chambersburg PA
CBHW020914160726
47993CB00005B/1974